James Russell Miller

Practical religion

A help for the common days

James Russell Miller

Practical religion
A help for the common days

ISBN/EAN: 9783743351875

Manufactured in Europe, USA, Canada, Australia, Japa

Cover: Foto ©ninafisch / pixelio.de

Manufactured and distributed by brebook publishing software (www.brebook.com)

James Russell Miller

Practical religion

CONTENTS.

CHAPTER	PAGE
I.—The Sweet Odor of Prayer	9
II.—The Blessing of Quietness	19
III.—"Ye have done It unto Me"	31
IV.—Transformed by Beholding	40
V.—Being Christians on Weekdays	50
VI.—Compensation in Life	59
VII.—The Cost of Being a Blessing	72
VIII.—Life as a Ladder	82
IX.—Seeds of Light	91
X.—Looking at the Right Side	104
XI.—For Better or Worse	116
XII.—"Doe ye Nexte Thynge"	126
XIII.—People as Means of Grace	139
XIV.—Shall we Worry?	150
XV.—A Word about Temper	161
XVI.—Forward, and not Back	173
XVII.—The Duty of Forgetting Sorrow	183

CHAPTER	PAGE
XVIII.—People who Fail	196
XIX.—Living Victoriously	209
XX.—Shut In	222
XXI.—Helpful People	235
XXII.—Tired Feet	247
XXIII.—Hands: A Study	259
XXIV.—Learning our Lessons	274
XXV.—Broken Lives	289
XXVI.—Coming to the End	305

OPENING WORDS.

This is not a volume of essays, but a collection of chapters written out of the author's own experience in the hope that they may do a little, at least, to make the path plainer for others. The book is all practical, without a line that is not intended to bear upon the actual life of the common days. It is not meant to show people an easy way of living—there is no easy way to live worthily—but it seeks to show why it is worth while to live earnestly, at whatever cost.

The book is designed to be a companion to *Week-Day Religion*, which has met with such wide and continued favor, and which appears to have been used by the Master to help many people over the hard places and up to a fuller, richer life. The hundreds of letters which have come from readers of that little book and of *Silent Times* have encouraged the author to prepare the present volume on the same line, and it is now sent forth in the hope that it likewise may have a ministry of encouragement, stimulus, comfort or strength in some lives of toil, care, struggle or sorrow.

J. R. M.

1334 Chestnut Street,
 Philadelphia.

PRACTICAL RELIGION.

I.

THE SWEET ODOR OF PRAYER.

> "When I look from my window at night,
> And the welkin above is all white,
>   All throbbing and panting with stars,
> Among the majestic is standing
> Sandolphon, the angel, expanding
>   His pinions in nebulous bars."
>
> LONGFELLOW.

TRUE prayer is fragrant to God. This was taught in the Old Testament in one of those emblem-lessons which, when read in the light of the gospel, mean so much. The golden incense-altar was the altar of prayer, just as the altar of burnt-offering was the altar of atonement and consecration. So every believing, loving heart is now a golden altar from which rise up to God sweet odors, bathing his very throne in fragrance.

In Saint John's Apocalyptic visions we find again

the emblem of incense as a feature of the heavenly state. The redeemed are represented as having in their hands "golden vials, full of odors, which are the prayers of saints." The meaning is not that the saints in glory offer up prayers to God. Rather, the thought seems to be that earth's supplications rise up into heaven as sweet incense—that while humble believers in this world are engaged in offering up prayers and supplications holy odors are wafted up before God. The picture seems designed to show us the heaven-side of earth's true worship —how our hearts' breathings of desire appear within the veil.

For one thing, it shows that the prayers of believers are not lost. Some people tell us there is no ear to hear when we speak our words of request and desire—that our petitions merely float off into the air, and that is the end of them. But here we get a glimpse inside heaven, and find our prayers caught and preserved in golden bowls. The thought is very beautiful.

In one of the psalms there is a similar hint regarding the tears of God's people. "Put thou my tears into thy bottle," cries David. In ancient times tear-bottles were sometimes used. When a man was in some sore distress, his friends would visit him, and, as he wept, would gather his tears and put them in a bottle, preserving them as sacred memorials of the event. Something like this appears to have been in David's thought when, in sore distress, he made the prayer, "Put thou my tears into thy bottle." The words suggest the precious truth that God does indeed take notice of all our sorrows, and that he treasures up the remembrance of our griefs. Our very tears he gathers, and as it were puts them in bottles, that they may not be lost or forgotten. This is one of those incidental allusions which show us how deeply God loves us and how tender is his care.

The picture of the golden bowls in heaven containing earth's prayers shows us like precious regard in the divine heart for the desires and supplications which believing ones put up to God. As they rise in holy breathings or in earnest cries he receives them—every sigh, every yearning, every pleading, every intercession of love, every heart-hunger —and puts them all into golden bowls, that none of them may be lost. Often our prayers may seem to remain long unanswered, for some blessings are so rich that they cannot be prepared for us in a day, but we may be sure that they are not lost nor forgotten. They are sacredly treasured and are always before God, and in due time they will receive gracious and wise answer.

The picture of the incense in the golden bowls in heaven shows, also, that the prayers of believers are very precious in God's sight. Burning incense made a most grateful and delicious perfume. Frequently in the Scriptures acceptable prayer is described as producing before God a sweet odor. "The Lord smelled a sweet savor" is the Bible way of saying that God was pleased with the worship rendered to him. There is an exquisite beauty in the thought that true prayer is fragrance to God as it rises from the golden altars of believing, loving hearts. The pleadings and supplications of his people on the earth are wafted up to him from lowly homes, from humble sanctuaries, from stately cathedrals, from sick-rooms and from the darkened chambers of sorrow as the breath of flowers is wafted to us from rich gardens and fragrant fields.

"There was a fitness, in the nature of things," says Dr. MacMillan, in a sermon on fragrance, "in incense being regarded as embodied prayer. Perfume is the breath of flowers, the sweetest expression of their inmost being, an exhalation of their very life. It is a sign of perfect purity, health and vigor, it is a symptom of full and joyous existence—for disease and decay and death yield, not pleasant but revolting odors—and, as such, fragrance is in nature what prayer is in the human world. Prayer is the breath of life, the expression of the soul's best, holiest and heavenliest aspirations, the symptom and token of its spiritual health. The natural counterparts of the prayers that rise from the closet and the sanctuary are to be found in the delicious breathings, sweetening all the air, from gardens of flowers, from clover-crofts or thymy hillsides or dim pine woods, and which seem to be grateful, unconscious acknowledgments from the heart of Nature for the timely blessings of the great world-covenant, dew to refresh and sunshine to quicken."

This thought is very beautiful—that the fragrance which rises from garden, field and wood is earth's prayer to God—but still more beautiful is the thought that true prayer is itself fragrance to God, that he delights in it as we delight in the perfume of sweet flowers.

There is also rich instruction for us concerning prayer in the way the incense was prepared and offered. For one thing, the ingredients for the incense were divinely prescribed: "The Lord said unto Moses, Take unto thee sweet spices, stacte, and onycha, and galbanum; these sweet spices with pure frankincense: of each shall there be a like weight: and thou shalt make it a perfume, a confection after the art of the apothecary, tempered together, pure and holy." The priest might not prepare any sort of mixture he pleased, but must use precisely what God had commanded. Any humanly-devised compound was an abomination. In like manner are there divine instructions concerning the elements that must mingle in acceptable prayer. It must be the prayer of faith. There must be penitence and contrition in it. It must contain thanksgiving and submission. It must be the kind of prayer that God has commanded or it will not rise to heaven as sweet incense.

The incense did not give forth its perfume until it was burning, and the only fire allowed to be used in kindling it was holy fire from the altar of burnt-offering. Mere cold words do not make prayer. There can be no incense-prayer without fire—the fire of love; and the fire must be kindled in the heart by coals from the altar of Calvary, by the love of God shed abroad by the Holy Spirit.

There is another rich suggestion concerning the incense as used in the ancient service. At the same time that the incense was burning on the golden altar within the sacrifice of atonement was burning on the altar of burnt-offering in the court without. The fire was carried from the sacrificial altar to kindle the incense. No other fire was permitted. The incense-odor would have been an abomination to God had not the smoke of the burnt-offering mingled and ascended with it. The teaching is that there will be no sweet savor in our prayers, no acceptableness before God, unless they are cleansed by the merits of Christ's atonement. We can approach God only in the precious name of Jesus Christ and in dependence on his sacrifice for us.

There is another Apocalyptic picture which has also an interesting suggestion: "Another angel came and stood over the altar, having a golden censer; and there was given unto him much incense, that he should offer it with the prayers of all saints upon the golden altar." The teaching is that the prayers of believers, even of the holiest saints, are not in themselves acceptable to God. At the best they are imperfect and defiled, because they come from imperfect and defiled hearts. The "much incense" that was added to the prayers of all the saints upon the golden altar was nothing less than the odors of the precious sacrifice and ever-availing intercession of Christ, "who hath given himself for us, an offering and a sacrifice to God, for a sweet-smelling savor."

If we would pray acceptably, it must be, therefore, in dependence on Jesus Christ, our High Priest in heaven, who shall take the petitions from our stained and unholy lips, cleanse them of their sin and fault and defilement, and then add to them the pure incense of his own holy offering and intercession and present them to the Father. That is what praying in the name of Christ means. Praying thus, our prayers are sweet odors to God. The thoughts and words that leave our hearts and lips spotted and unholy, without any beauty or sweetness, when they come up before God have become precious perfumes.

The old Talmudic legend of Sandolphon, the angel of prayer, suggests a like wonderful transformation as taking place in the human petitions that go up from earth's lowly places and from unholy lips to heaven's gate. Longfellow has wrought the beautiful legend into verse, telling of Sandolphon, the angel of prayer—

> "How erect at the outermost gates
> Of the City Celestial he waits,
>   With his feet on the ladder of light,

THE SWEET ODOR OF PRAYER.

> That, crowded with angels unnumbered,
> By Jacob was seen as he slumbered
>   Alone in the desert at night."

Then the poet goes on to tell how serene in the rapturous throng, unmoved among the other angels,

> "the deathless
> Sandolphon stands listening breathless
>   To sounds that ascend from below—
>
> "From the spirits on earth that adore,
> From the souls that entreat and implore
>   In the fervor and passion of prayer;
> From the hearts that are broken with losses,
> And weary with dragging the crosses
>   Too heavy for mortals to bear.
>
> "And he gathers the prayers as he stands,
> And they change into flowers in his hands—
>   Into garlands of purple and red;
> And beneath the great arch of the portal,
> Through the streets of the City Immortal,
>   Is wafted the fragrance they shed."

This old rabbinical legend, though but a legend, surely does not exaggerate the truth about the acceptableness of prayer. Earth's sighs of faith and love and heart-hunger, though without beauty or sweetness or worthiness in themselves, float upward and are caught by the listening Intercessor, and in his holy, **radiant hands,** bearing yet the nail-marks, are transformed **into lovely** and **fragrant** flowers, and pour their **perfume** throughout **all** heaven's glorious mansions.

II.

THE BLESSING OF QUIETNESS.

"Drop Thy still dews of quietness
   Till all our strivings cease;
Take from our souls the strain and stress,
And let our ordered lives confess
   The beauty of thy peace."

WHITTIER.

QUIETNESS, like mercy, is twice blessed: it blesseth him that is quiet, and it blesseth the man's friends and neighbors. Talk is good in its way. "There is a time to speak," but there is also "a time to be silent," and in silence many of life's sweetest benedictions come.

An Italian proverb says, "He that speaks doth sow; he that holds his peace doth reap." We all know the other saying which rates speech as silver and silence as gold. There are in the Scriptures, too, many strong persuasives to quietness and many exhortations against noise. It was prophesied of the Christ: "He shall not cry, nor lift up, nor cause his voice to be heard in the street." As we read the Gospels we see that our Lord's whole life was a fulfillment of this ancient prophecy. He made no noise in the world. He did his work without excitement, without parade, without confusion. He wrought as the light works — silently, yet pervasively and with resistless energy.

Quietness is urged, too, on Christ's followers. "Study to be quiet," writes an apostle. "Busybodies" the same apostle exhorts that "with quietness they work." Prayers are to be made for rulers "that we may lead a quiet and peaceable life." Another apostle, writing to Christian women, speaks of their true adornment as being "the ornament of a meek and quiet spirit, which is in the sight of God of great price." Solomon rates quietness in a home far above the best of luxuries:

"Better is a dry morsel and quietness therewith,
Than an house full of feasting with strife."

A prophet declares the secret of power in these words: "In quietness and confidence shall be your strength;" and likewise says, "The work of righteousness shall be peace, and the effect of righteousness quietness and assurance for ever." It is set down also as one of the blessings of God's people that they shall dwell in "quiet resting-places."

These are but a few of very many scriptural words concerning quietness, but they are enough to indicate several lessons that we may profitably consider.

We should be quiet toward God. The expression "Rest in the Lord," in one of the Psalms, is in the margin "Be silent to the Lord." We are not to speak back to God when he speaks to us. We are not to reason with him or dispute with him, but are to bow in silent and loving acquiescence before him: "Be still, and know that I am God." It is in those providences which cut sorely into our lives and require sacrifice and loss on our part that we are specially called to this duty. There is a pathetic illustration of silence to God in the case of Aaron when his sons had offered strange fire, and had died before the Lord for their disobedience and sacrilege. The record says, "And Aaron held his peace." He even made no natural human outcry of grief. He accepted the terrible penalty as unquestionably just, and bowed in the acquiescence of faith.

This silence to God should be our attitude in all times of trial when God's ways with us are bitter and painful. Why should we complain at anything that our Father may do? We have no right to utter a word of **murmuring,** for he is our sovereign Lord, and our simple duty is instant, unquestioning **submission.** Then we have no reason to complain, for we know **that all** God's **dealings with** us are in loving wisdom. His will is always best for us, **whatever** sacrifice or suffering **it may cost.**

> "Thou layest thy hand on the fluttering heart,
>   And sayest, "Be still!"
> The silence and shadow are only a part
>   **Of thy** sweet will;
> Thy presence is with me, and where thou art
>   I **fear no ill.**"

We should train ourselves to be quiet also toward **men.** There are times when we should speak **and** when words are mighty and full of blessing. Universal dumbness would not be a boon to the world. Among the most beneficent of God's gifts to us is **the** power of speech. And we are **to** use our tongues. There are some people who are altogether too quiet in certain directions and toward certain persons. There is no place where good **words are** more fitting than between husband and wife, yet there are husbands and wives who pass weeks and months together in almost unbroken silence. They will travel long journeys side by **side in** the railway-car, and utter scarcely a word in the whole distance. They will walk to and from church, and neither will speak. In the home-life they will pass whole days with nothing more in the form of speech between them than an indifferent remark about the weather, a formal inquiry and a monosyllabic answer.

"According to Milton, Eve kept silence in Eden to hear her husband talk," said a gentleman to a lady, adding in a melancholy tone, "Alas! there have been no Eves since!"—"Because," quickly retorted the lady, "there have been no husbands worth listening to." Perhaps the retort was just. Husbands certainly ought to have something to say when they come into their homes from the busy world outside. They are usually genial enough in the circles of business or politics or literature, and are able to talk so as to interest others. Ought they not to seek to be as genial in their own homes, especially toward their own wives? Most women, too, are able to talk in general society. Why, then, should a wife fall into such a mood of silence the moment she and her husband are alone? It was Franklin who wisely said, "As we must account for every idle word, so must we for every idle silence." We must not forget that silence may be sadly overdone, especially in homes.

There are other silences that are also to be deplored. People keep in their hearts unspoken the kindly words they might utter—ought to utter—in the ears of the weary, the soul-hungry and the sorrowing about them. The ministry of good words is one of wondrous power, yet many of us are wretched misers with our gold and silver coin of speech. Is any miserliness so mean? Ofttimes we allow hearts to starve close beside us, though in our very hands we have abundance to feed them. One who attends the funeral of any ordinary man and listens to what his neighbors have to say about him as they stand by his coffin will hear enough kind words spoken to have brightened whole years of his life. But how was it when the man was living, toiling and struggling among these very people? Ah! they were not so faithful then with their grateful, appreciative words. They were too quiet toward him then. Silence was overdone.

Quietness is carried too far when it makes us disloyal to the hearts that crave our words of love and sympathy. But there is a quietness toward others which all should cultivate. There are many words spoken which ought never to pass the door of the lips. There are people who seem to exercise no restraint whatever on their speech. They allow every passing thought or feeling to take form in words. They never think what the effect of their words will be—how they will fly like arrows shot by some careless marksman and will pierce hearts they were never meant to hurt. Thus friendships are broken and injuries are inflicted which can never be repaired. Careless words are for ever making grief and sorrow in tender spirits. We pity the dumb whom sometimes we meet. Dumbness is more blessed by far than speech if all we can do with our marvelous gift is to utter bitter, angry, abusive or sharp, cutting words.

> "I heedlessly opened the cage
>   And suffered my bird to go free,
> And, though I besought it with tears to return,
>   It nevermore came back to me.
> It nests in the wildwood and heeds not my call;
> Oh, the bird once at liberty who can enthrall?
>
> "I hastily opened my lips
>   And uttered a word of disdain
> That wounded a friend, and for ever estranged
>   A heart I would die to regain.
> But the bird once at liberty who can enthrall?
> And the word that's once spoken, oh who can recall?"

Rose Terry Cooke in one of her poems—"Unreturning"—shows in very strong phrase the irreparableness of the harm done or the hurt given by

unkind words. Flowers fade, but there will be more flowers another year—just as sweet ones, too, as those that are gone. **Snow** melts and disappears, but it will snow again. The crystals of dew on leaf and grass-**blade** vanish when the sun rises, but to-morrow morning there will be other dewdrops as brilliant as those which are lost. But words once **uttered can** never be said over to be changed, nor **can** they ever be gotten back.

> "Never shall thy spoken word
> **Be** again unsaid, unheard.
> **Well its** work the utterance **wrought,**
> **Woe** or weal—what'er it brought:
> **Once for** all the rune **is** read,
> **Once for all the** judgment said.
> Though it pierced, **a** poisoned spear,
> Through the soul thou holdest dear,
> Though **it** quiver, fierce and deep,
> Through some stainless spirit's sleep;
> Idle, **vain, the flying sting**
> That a passing rage **might** bring,
> Speech **shall give** it fangs of steel,
> Utterance all **its** barb reveal.

> "Give thy tears of blood and fire,
> Pray with pangs of mad desire,
> Offer life and soul and all,
> That one sentence to recall;
> Wrestle with its fatal wrath,
> Chase with flying feet its path;

> Rue it all thy lingering days,
> Hide it deep with love and praise,—
> Once for all thy word is sped;
> None evade it but the dead.
> All thy travail will be vain:
> Spoken words come not again."

Another kind of common talk that had better be repressed into complete silence is the miserable gossip which forms so large a part—let us confess it and deplore it—of ordinary parlor conversation. Few appreciative and kindly things are spoken of absent ones, but there is no end to criticism, snarling and backbiting. The most unsavory bits of scandal are served with relish, and no character is proof against the virulence and maliciousness of the tongues that chatter on as innocently and glibly as if they were telling sweet stories of good. It certainly would be infinitely better if all this kind of speech were reduced to utter silence. It were better that the ritual of fashion prescribed some sort of a dumb pantomime for social calls, receptions and *tête-à-têtes* in place of any conversation whatsoever if there is nothing to be talked about but the faults and foibles and the characters and doings of absent people. Will not some new Peter the Hermit preach a crusade against backbiting? Shall we not have a new annual "week of prayer" to cry to God for the gift of silence when **we** have nothing **good or** true or beautiful **to say**? No victories should **be more** heroically battled **for or more** thankfully recorded than victories of silence when we are tempted to speak unhallowed words of others.

Silence is better, also, than any words of bickering and strife. There is no surer, better way of preventing quarrels than by the firm restraining of speech. "A soft answer turneth away wrath;" but if we cannot command the "soft answer" when another person is angry, the second-best thing is not to speak **at all**. "Grievous words stir up anger." Many a long, fierce strife that has produced untold pain and heartburning would **never have** been anything more than a momentary flash of **anger** if one of the parties had practiced **the** holy art of silence.

Some **one** tells of the following arrangement **which** worked successfully in preventing family quarrels: "You see, sir," said an old man, speaking of a couple in his neighborhood who lived in perfect harmony, "they had agreed between themselves that whenever he came home a little *contrairy* and out of temper he would **wear** his hat on the back of his head, and **then** she never said a word; and if she came in a little cross and crooked, she would throw her shawl over her left shoulder, and he never said a word." So they never quarreled.

He who has learned to be silent spares himself ofttimes from confusion. Many men have owed their reputation for great wisdom quite as much to their silence as to their speech. They have not spoken the many foolish things of the glib talker, and have uttered only few and well-considered words. Says Carlyle, denouncing the rapid verbiage of shallow praters, "Even triviality and imbecility that can sit silent—how respectable are they in comparison!" An English writer gives the story of a groom wedded to a lady of wealth. He was in constant fear of being ridiculed by his wife's guests. A clergyman said to him, "Wear a black coat and hold your tongue." The new husband followed the advice, and soon was considered one of the finest gentlemen in the country. The power of keeping quiet would be worth a great deal to many people whose tongues are for ever betraying their ignorance and revealing their true character.

All true culture is toward the control and the restraining of speech. Christian faith gives a quietness which in itself is one of life's holiest benedictions. It gives the quietness of peace—a quietness which the wildest storms cannot disturb, which is a richer possession than all the world's wealth or power.

"Study to be quiet." The lesson may be hard to many of us, but it is well worth all the cost of learning. It brings strength and peace to the heart. Speech is good, but ofttimes silence is better. **He** who has learned to hold his tongue is a greater conqueror than the warrior who subdues an empire. The power to be silent under provocations and wrongs and in the midst of danger and alarms is the power of the noblest, royalest victoriousness.

III.

YE HAVE DONE IT UNTO ME.

"Without a recognition
  You passed Him yesterday—
Jostled aside, unhelped, his mute petition—
  And calmly went your way.

"Oh, dreamers, dreaming that your faith is keeping
  All service free from blot,
Christ daily walks your streets, sick, suffering, weeping,
  And ye perceive him not."

MARGARET J. PRESTON.

THOSE certainly seem strange words which our Lord says he will speak on the judgment-day to the multitudes before him. We are taught elsewhere that faith in Christ is the vital thing in determining one's eternity, yet Christ himself, in portraying the judgment, says not a word about believing on him or confessing him. Those who are welcomed to the kingdom prepared for them from the foundation of the world are those who have fed the hungry, given drink to the thirsty, covered the shivering and cold, visited the sick and cared for the prisoner. Are we, then, to reverse our cherished evangelical belief that men are saved by faith, and not by works? May we not say that the good deeds here described are the fruit of grace in the heart? We are not saved by our own ministries of love; but if we are saved, these are the acts we will perform.

Our Lord's words show us the kind of Christian life we should live in this world. We say we love Christ, and he tells us that we must show our affection for him in kindnesses to his friends. Then he goes farther and puts himself before us, to be served and helped as if personally in every needy and suffering one who comes to us: "I was an hungred, and ye gave me meat. . . . I was sick, and ye visited me."—"When saw we thee an hungred, and fed thee? . . . When saw we thee sick . . . and came unto thee?"—"Inasmuch as ye have done it unto one of the least of these my brethren, ye have done it unto me."

There is something inexpressibly beautiful in the revelation which these words of our Lord bring to our hearts. Christ himself is ever standing before us, appealing to us for love, for sympathy, for ministry. How all human lives about us are transfigured by this word which tells us that in the lowliest Jesus himself waits! No wonder this sweet truth has wrought itself into numberless legends beautiful telling how abject forms, when served in the Master's name in time of need, suddenly changed into radiant loveliness, revealing themselves as Jesus the glorious One. There is the legend of St. Christopher, who in carrying the little child over the wild stream in the darkness and the storm found that he was bearing the Christ himself. There is the story of Elizabeth of Hungary, whose kindness to the sick and the poor was so great. Once she brought a leprous child to her palace and laid it in her own bed, because there was no other place to lay it. Her husband heard of it, and came in some displeasure and drew down the cover of the bed to see if the object concealed there was really so loathsome as he had heard, and, lo! instead of the festering and leprous body, he saw the Saviour radiant with glory, and turned awe-stricken, and yet glad. Then the legend of the Holy Grail is familiar to all. The Holy Grail was the cup from which Jesus drank at the Last Supper. According to the tradition, this cup was lost, and it was a favorite enterprise of the knights of Arthur's court to go in quest of it. One of the most delightful of these stories is that which Mr. Lowell tells in his "Sir Launfal." Far away over cold mountains **and through** fierce storms rode **the** brave young knight till youth turned to age and his hair was gray. At last, after a vain search, he **turned homeward, an** old man, bent, worn out and **frail,** with garments thin and **spare.** As he drew on there lay a leper, lank and wan, cowering before **him.** "For Christ's sweet sake, I **beg an** alms," the leper said. Sir Launfal saw in the beggar an image of Jesus.

> "He parted **in twain** his single crust,
> He broke **the ice** on the streamlet's brink,
> And gave the leper to eat and drink.". . .

Suddenly a light shone round about the place.

> "The leper no longer crouched at his side,
> But stood before him glorified,
> Shining and tall and fair and straight
> **As** the pillar that stood by the Beautiful Gate."

Sweetly now he spoke as the knight listened :

> "In many climes, without avail,
> **Thou** hast spent thy life for the Holy Grail;
> Behold, **it** is here—this cup which thou
> Didst fill at the streamlet for me but now;
> **This crust** is my body broken for thee,
> This water His blood that died on the tree;
> The Holy Supper is kept indeed
> **In** whatso we share with another's need—

Not what we give, but what we share,
For the gift without the giver is bare:
Who gives himself with his alms feeds three—
Himself, his hungering neighbor and me."

A popular author has written a tender little story showing how these opportunities for serving Christ fill the plain, common days of the lowliest life. A poor man whose heart God had touched dreamt one night that one called him by name. As he listened he heard also these words: "Look to-morrow on the street. I am coming." He knew not the meaning of his singular dream, yet his heart was strangely warm all the day. He wrought in his little shop and watched the people as they went by. By and by came an old soldier with a shovel, and began to clear away the snow from the sidewalk. The shoemaker saw him, and observed, at length, that the soldier was very weary. Going to the door, he invited him to come in and have some warm tea. The exhausted man gratefully accepted the invitation, and, greatly refreshed by the kindness, at length went his way.

Later a woman in poor garb and carrying a child stopped before the window. Both mother and child were thinly clad, and the child was crying. Again the shoemaker opened his door, called to the woman and bade her come into his shop, where it was warm. The astonished mother obeyed, and, sitting by the stove, told her story of hunger and want. Soon the old man brought food for her and her child, sending them forth warmed and fed, and with some money to provide for further need.

Next it was an old apple-woman who drew the shoemaker's attention. A rude boy was annoying her. Again the kind-hearted man went out of his shop and acted as peacemaker and friend.

Thus the day passed. At his work Martuin remembered continually the vision of the night before, and watched all the hours for the appearing of Him who had promised to come. He saw no bright presence, but a number of poor people he helped and comforted.

Night came, and the shoemaker took down his New Testament to read. Again he seemed to hear some one stepping behind him, and there was a voice in his ear: " Martuin, did you not recognize me?"—" Whom?" asked the old man.—" Me," repeated the voice. " It is I;" and the old soldier Martuin had fed and warmed stepped from the shadows, smiled and vanished.—" And this is I," said the voice again, while from the darkness the woman and her child appeared, smiled and vanished.—"And this is I," again spoke the voice, and the poor apple-woman stepped forward, beamed a kindly look and passed out of sight.

The old shoemaker put on his glasses and began to read where his New Testament chanced to open. At the top of the page he read: "For I was an hungred, and ye gave me meat: I was thirsty, and ye gave me drink: I was a stranger, and ye took me in." Then a little farther down he read again: "Inasmuch as ye have done it unto one of the least of these my brethren, ye have done it unto me."

"Then Martuin understood," says the little book, "that his dream did not deceive him—that the Saviour really called on him that day, and that he really received him."

The other side of this truth we must also notice: "I was an hungred, and ye gave me no meat; I was thirsty, and ye gave me no drink. . . . Inasmuch as ye did it not to one of the least of these, ye did it not to me." The Lord Jesus is always standing before us and always coming up to us in the persons of his poor and needy ones. And what if we pay no heed to him? What if we coldly turn him away?

There is another legend which illustrates this

side of the lesson. Once an angel whispered to a good woman in the morning that her Lord was coming to her house that day. She made ready for him with loving care, and eagerly watched all day for his coming. At twilight a poor little child came to her door and craved shelter for the night, but the woman was thinking so much of her Lord that she only gave the child a little money and sent him on into the gathering darkness. But as he turned away the child grew fair and beautiful, and as he vanished in a flood of glory the good woman heard the words, "Adine, behold thy Lord!" He had come, had not been recognized, had been treated coldly, and had passed beyond recall, vanishing as he revealed himself.

The lesson is intensely practical; it touches all our common daily life. If we neglect one of Christ's little ones, we shall hear on judgment-day, "I was hungry, and you gave me no bread. I was shivering in the cold, and you clothed me not. I was a homeless stranger at your door, and you showed me no pity." It seems a little thing to treat with neglect, or even with unkindness, some needy one. We cannot see how it matters to us, what claim the person has on us, why we need turn aside from our own way to do anything.

This picture of the final judgment helps us to see why it does matter, that the person really has a claim on us, that it is indeed the same as if it were Jesus himself who was in need.

It must be noticed that it will be the things men have failed to do which shall turn the scales on the great trial-day. We must meet in judgment our neglects as well as our sinful acts. Those who are sent to the left hand are not described as great sinners. They have not been cruel, inhuman or unjust. They are not charged with having wronged or injured one of Christ's little ones. Only neglects are in the indictment. They have seen little ones hungry, and have not fed them; thirsty, and have not given them the cup of cold water; shivering in the cold, and have not clothed them; sick, and have not visited them. They have merely "passed by on the other side" when they have seen human need in their way which they might have relieved or sorrow which they might have comforted.

We need to walk reverently and thoughtfully through life, not jostling roughly against the meanest person we meet, not looking coldly on the poorest that comes to our doors, lest in the judgment we may find that we have neglected to show kindness to our blessed Lord.

IV.

TRANSFORMED BY BEHOLDING.

"Renew thine image, **Lord,** in me;
Lowly and gentle may I be:
No charms but these to thee are dear;
No anger mayst thou ever find,
No pride in my unruffled mind,
But faith and heaven-born peace be there."

GERHARDT.

THE deepest yearning of every true Christian life is to be like Christ. But what is Christ like? In the fourth century the empress **Constantine** sent to Eusebius, begging him to send **her** a likeness of the Saviour. "What do you mean," Eusebius asked in reply, "by a likeness of Christ? Not, of course, the image of him as he is truly and unchangeably; not his human nature glorified, as it was at the Transfiguration. . . . Since we confess that our Saviour is God and Lord, **we** prepare ourselves to see him as God; and if, **in** addition to this hope, you set high value on images **of** the Saviour, what better artist can there be than the God-word himself?" Thus he referred the empress to the New Testament for the only true picture of Christ.

When one turned to Jesus himself and gave utterance to his heart's yearning in the prayer, "Show us the Father," the answer was, "Look at me. He that hath seen me hath seen the Father." When we turn the pages of the Gospels and look upon the life of Christ as it is portrayed there in sweet gentleness, in radiant purity, in tender compassion, in patience under injury and wrong, in dying on the cross to save the guilty, we see the only true picture of Christ there is in this world. There is an old legend that Jesus left his likeness on the handkerchief the pitying woman gave him to wipe the sweat from his face as he went out to die; yet this is but a legend, and the only image he really left in the world when he went away is that which we have in the gospel pages. Artists paint their conceptions of that blessed face, but there is more true Christlikeness in a single verse in the New Testament than in all the faces of the Saviour that artists have ever drawn; so we can even now look upon the holy beauty of Christ.

One of John Bunyan's characters is made to say, "Wherever I have seen the print of his shoe in the earth, there **have I** coveted **to set** my foot too." To walk **where our** Master walked, to do the things he did, **to** have the same mind that was in him, to **be** like him, is the highest aim **of** every worthy Christian life; and when this longing springs up **in our** heart and we ask, "What is he like that **I may** imitate his beauty? Where can I find his portrait?" we have but to turn to the pages of the gospel, and there our eyes can behold Him who is altogether lovely—in whom all glory and beauty shine.

No sooner do we begin to behold the fair face that looks out at us from the gospel chapters than a great hope springs up in our hearts. We can become like Jesus. Indeed, if we are God's children, we *shall* become like him. We are foreordained to **be** conformed to his image. It matters not how faintly the divine beauty glimmers now in **our** soiled and imperfect lives: some **day** we shall be like him. As we struggle here with imperfections and infirmities, with scarcely one trace of Christ-**likeness** yet apparent in **our** life, we still may say, when we **catch** glimpses of the glorious loveliness **of** Christ, "Some day I shall be like that."

But how may we grow into the Christlikeness of Christ? Not merely by our own strugglings and strivings. **We know** what we want **to be; but when we try to** lift **our** own lives up to the **beauty** we see and admire, we find ourselves weighted down. We cannot make ourselves Christlike by any efforts of our own. Nothing less than a divine **power** is sufficient to produce this transformation in our human nature.

The Scripture describes the process. Beholding the glory **of** the **Lord,** we are changed into the image **of the** glory—that is, we are to find the likeness **of Christ, and** are to look upon it and ponder it, gazing intently and lovingly upon it, and as we gaze we are transformed and grow like Christ; something of the glory **of** his face passes into our dull faces and stays there, shining out in us.

We know well the influence on our own natures **of** things we look upon familiarly and constantly. A man sits before the photographer's camera, and the image of his face prints itself on the glass in the darkened chamber of the instrument. Something like this process is going on continually in every human soul. But the man is the camera, and the things that pass before him cast their images within him and print their pictures on his soul. Every strong, pure human friend with whom we move in sympathetic association does something toward the transforming of our character into his own image. The familiar scenes and circumstances amid which we live and move are in a very real sense photographed upon our souls. Refinement without us tends to the refining of our spirits. The same is true of all evil influences. Bad companionships degrade those who choose them. Thus even of human lives about us it is true that, beholding them, we are transformed into the same image.

But it is true in a far higher sense of the beholding of Christ. It is not merely a brief glance now and then that is here implied, not the turning of the eye toward him for a few hurried moments in the early morning or in the late evening, but a constant, loving and reverent beholding of him through days and years till his image burns itself upon the soul. If we thus train our heart's eyes to look at Christ, we shall be transformed into his image.

"Beholding we are changed." The verb is passive. We do not produce the change. The marble can never carve itself into the lovely figure that floats in the artist's mind: the transformation must be wrought with patience by the sculptor's own hands. We cannot change ourselves into the image of Christ's glory: we are changed. The work is wrought in us by the divine Spirit. We simply look upon the image of the Christ, and its blessed light streams in upon us and prints its own radiant glory upon our hearts. We have nothing to do but to keep our eyes fixed upon the mirrored beauty as the flowers hold up their faces toward the sun, and the transformation is divinely wrought in us. It is not wrought instantaneously. At first there are but dimmest glimmerings of the likeness of Christ. We cannot in a single day learn all the long, hard lessons of patience, meekness, unselfishness, humility, joy and peace. Little by little the change is wrought, and the beauty comes out as we continue to gaze upon Christ. Little by little the glory flows into our lives from the radiant face of the Master, and flows out again through our dull lives, transforming them.

Even though but little seems to come from our yearnings and struggles after Christlikeness, God honors the yearning and the striving, and while we sit in the shadows of weariness, disheartened with our failures, he carries on the work within us, and with his own hands produces the divine beauty in our souls. There is a pleasant legend of Michael Angelo. He was engaged on a painting, but grew weary and discouraged while his work was yet incomplete, and at length fell asleep. Then while he slept an angel came, and, seizing the brush that had dropped from the tired artist's fingers, finished the picture,

> "Wrought the wondrous work—a love-thought carried
> Into colors fit and fair, completed."

Angelo awoke at length, affrighted that he had slept and foregone his task in self-indulgence, but, looking at his canvas, his heart was thrilled with joy and his soul uplifted beyond measure, for he saw that while he had slept his picture had been finished, and that it had been

> "painted fairer
> Far than any picture of his making
> In the past, with tint and touch diviner,
> And a light of God above it breaking."

So it is with all who truly long and strive after the heavenly likeness. Faint and discouraged, they think they are making no progress, no growth toward the divine image, but in the very time of their faintness and disheartenment, "when human hands are weary folded," God's Spirit comes and silently fashions the beauty in their souls. When they awake, they shall see the work finished, and shall be satisfied in Christ's likeness.

There is great comfort in this for many of the

Father's weary children who earnestly long to become like the Master, and who struggle without ceasing to attain the divine image, but who seem to themselves never to make any progress. God is watching them, sees their strivings, is not impatient with their failures, and in the hours of quiet will send his angel to help them. Perhaps the very hours of their deepest discouragement may be the hours when they are growing the most, for then God works most helpfully in them.

There is still another thought. The Revised Version makes a change in the reading of the words about beholding the glory of the Lord, and puts them in this way: "We all, with unveiled face, reflecting as a mirror the glory of the Lord, are transformed into the same image." According to this rendering we too become mirrors. We gaze upon the glory of the Lord, and as we gaze the glory streams upon us, and there is an image of Christ reflected and mirrored in us. Then others, looking upon us, see the image of Christ in our lives.

We look into a little pool of still water at night and see the stars in it, or by day and see the blue sky, the passing clouds and the bright sun high in the heavens. So we look upon Christ in loving, adoring faith, and the glory shines down into our soul. Then our neighbors and friends about us look at us, see our character, watch our conduct, observe our disposition and temper and all the play of our life, and as they behold us they perceive the image of Christ in us. We are the mirrors, and in us men see the beauty of the Lord.

A little child was thinking about the unseen Christ to whom she prayed, and came to her mother with the question, "Is Jesus like anybody I know?" The question was not an unreasonable one: it was one to which the child should have received the answer "Yes." Every true disciple of Christ ought to be an answer—in some sense, at least—to the child's inquiry. Every little one ought to see Christ's beauty mirrored in its mother's face. Every Sabbath-school teacher's character should reflect some tracings of the eternal Love on which the scholars may gaze. Whoever looks upon the life of any Christian should see in it at once the reflection of the beauty of Christ.

Of course the mirroring never can be perfect. Muddy pools give only dim reflections of the blue sky and the bright sun. Too often our lives are like muddy pools. A broken mirror gives a very imperfect reflection of the face that looks into it.

Many times our lives are broken, shattered mirrors and show only little fragments of the glory they are intended to reflect. If one holds the back of a mirror toward the sun, there will be in it no reflection of the orb of day; the mirror's face must be turned toward the object whose image one wants to catch. If we would have Christ mirrored in our lives, we must turn and hold our faces always Christward. If we continue ever beholding the glory, gazing upon it, we shall be mirrors reflecting Him into whose face we gaze. Then those who look upon our lives will see in us a dim image at least, a little picture, of Christ.

V.
BEING CHRISTIANS ON WEEKDAYS.

> "There are in this loud stunning tide
>   Of human care and crime
> With whom the melodies abide
>   Of th' everlasting chime—
> Who carry music in their heart,
>   Through dusky lane and wrangling mart,
> Plying their daily task with busier feet
> Because their secret souls a holy strain repeat."
>
> KEBLE.

HOW to carry our religion into all parts of our life is the question which perplexes many of us. It is not hard to be good on the quiet Sabbaths, when all the holy influences of the sanctuary and of the Christian home are about us. It is not hard, in such an atmosphere, to think of God, and to yield ourselves to the impact of the divine Spirit. It is easy then to accept the promises and allow them to twine themselves about our weakness, like a mother's arms about feeble infancy. Most of us have little trouble with doubts and fears or with temptations and trials while sitting in the peaceful retreats into which the Sabbath leads us.

Our trouble is in carrying this sweet, holy, restful life out into the weekday world of toil, anxiety, strife and pain. Ofttimes with Monday morning we lose all the Sabbath calm and resume again the old experience of restless distraction. The restraints of godliness lose their power, and the enthusiasm for holy living, so strong yesterday, dies out in the midst of the world's chilling influences, and we drop back into the old habitudes and creep along again in the old dusty ways.

The Sabbath has lifted us up for a day, but has not power to hold us up in sustained elevation of soul. The duties we saw so clearly and so firmly determined to do while sitting in the sanctuary we do not feel pressing upon us to-day with half the urgency of yesterday. Our high resolves and our excellent intentions have proved only like the morning cloud and the early dew; so our religion becomes a sort of luxury to us—a bright unreal dream only which for one day in seven breaks into the worldliness and the self-seeking of our humdrum lives, giving us a period of elevation, but no permanent uplifting. It is only as when one climbs up out of a valley into the pure air of a mountain-top for one hour, and then creeps down again and toils on as before amid the mists and in the deep shadows, but carrying none of the mountain's inspiration or of the mountain's splendor with him back into the valley.

Yet such a life has missed altogether the meaning of the religion of Christ, which is not designed to furnish merely a system of Sabbath oases across the desert of life, with nothing between but sand and glare. Both its precepts and its blessings are for all the days. He who worships God only on Sabbaths, and then ignores him or disobeys him on weekdays, really has no true religion. We are perpetually in danger of bisecting our life, calling one portion of it religious and the other secular. Young people, when they enter the church, are earnestly urged to Christian duty, and the impression made upon them is that Christian duty means reading the Bible and praying every day, attending upon the public means of grace, taking active part in some of the associations, missionary or charitable, which belong to the Church, and in private and personal ways striving to bring others to Christ.

Now, important as these things are, they are by no means all the religious duties of any young Christian, and it is most fallacious teaching that emphasizes them as though they were all.

Religion recognizes no bisecting into sacred and secular. "Whether therefore ye eat, or drink, or whatsoever ye do, do all to the glory of God." It is just as much a part of Christian duty to do one's weekday work well as it is to pray well. "I must be about my Father's business," said Jesus in the dawn of youth; and what do we find him doing after this recognition of his duty? Not preaching nor teaching, but taking up the common duties of common life and putting all his soul into them. He found the Father's business in his earthly home, in being a dutiful child subject to his parents, in being a diligent pupil in the village school, and later in being a conscientious carpenter. He did not find religion too spiritual, too transcendental, for weekdays. His devotion to God did not take him out of his natural human relationships into any realm of mere sentiment: it only made him all the more loyal to the duties of his place in life.

We ought to learn the lesson. Religion is intensely practical. Only so far as it dominates one's life is it real. We must get the commandments down from the Sinaitic glory amid which they were first graven on stone by the finger of God and give them a place in the hard, dusty paths of earthly toil and struggle. We must get them off the tables of stone and have them written on the walls of **our own** hearts. We must bring the Golden **Rule** down from **its** bright setting in the teaching of our **Lord** and **get** it wrought into our daily, actual life.

We say in creed, confession and prayer that we love God, and he tells **us**, if we do, to show **it by** loving our fellow-men, since professed love to God which is not thus manifested is not love at all. **We** talk about our consecration; if there is anything genuine in consecration, it bends our wills to **God's**, it leads us to loyalty that costs, it draws our lives **to lowly ministry.** "One secret act of self-denial," **says a** thoughtful writer, "**one** sacrifice **of** inclination to duty, is worth all the mere good thoughts, warm feelings, passionate prayers, in which idle people indulge themselves."

> "Faith's meanest deed more favor **bears**
> Where hearts and wills are weighed
> **Than** brightest transports, choicest prayers,
> Which **bloom** their **hour** and fade."

We are **too apt to** imagine **that** holiness consists in mere good feeling toward God. **It does not**: it consists in obedience in heart and life to the divine requirements. **To be holy is, first, to be set** apart for God and devoted to God's service: "The **Lord** hath set apart him that **is** godly for himself;"

but if we are set apart for God in this sense, it necessarily follows that we must live for God. We belong wholly to him, and any use of our life in any other service is sacrilege, as if one would rob the very altar of its smoking sacrifice to gratify one's common hunger. Our hands are God's, and can fitly be used only in doing his work; our feet are God's, and may be employed only in walking in his ways and running his errands; our lips are God's, and should speak words only that honor him and bless others; our hearts are God's, and must not be profaned by thoughts and affections that are not pure.

Ideal holiness is no vague sentiment: it is intensely practical. It is nothing less than the bringing of every thought and feeling and act into obedience to Christ. We are quite in danger of leaving out the element of obedience in our conception of Christian living. If we do this, our religion loses its strength and grandeur and becomes weak, nerveless and forceless. As one has said, " Let us be careful how we cull from the gospel such portions as are congenial, forge God's signature to the excerpt, and apply the fiction as a delusive anodyne to our violated consciences. The beauties and graces of the gospel are all flung upon a background of

requirements as inflexible as Sinai and the granite. Christ built even his glory out of obedience."

Now, it is the weekday life, under the stress and **the** strain of temptation, far more than the Sunday life, beneath the gentle warmth of its favoring conditions, that really puts our religion to the test and shows what power there is in it. Not how well we sing and pray nor how devoutly we worship on the Lord's day, but how well we live, how loyally **we** obey the commandments, how faithfully we attend **to** all our duties, on the other days, tell what **manner of** Christians we really are.

Nor can we be faithful toward God and ignore **our** human relationships. "**It is** impossible," says one, " for us to live in fellowship with God without holiness in all the duties of life. These things act and react on each other. Without a diligent and faithful obedience to the calls and claims of others **upon** us, our religious profession is simply dead. We cannot go from strife, breaches and angry words **to God.** Selfishness, an imperious will, want of sympathy with the sufferings and sorrows of other **men,** neglect of charitable offices, suspicions, hard **censures of** those with whom our lot is cast, will miserably darken our own hearts and hide the face **of God from us.**"

The one word which defines and describes all relative duties is the word *love*. Many people understand religion to include honesty, truthfulness, justice, purity, but do not think of it as including just as peremptorily unselfishness, thoughtfulness, kindness, patience, good temper and courtesy. We are commanded to put away lying, but in the same paragraph, and with equal urgency, we are enjoined to let all bitterness, wrath, anger, clamor and evil-speaking be put away, and to be kind one to another, tender-hearted, forgiving one another. The law of love in all its most delicate shades of application to spirit, word, act and manner is the law of all true Christian living.

Thus the religion of the Sabbath, like a precious perfume, must pervade all the days of the week. Its spirit of holiness and reverence must flow down into all the paths of every-day life. Its voices of hope and joy must become inspirations in all our cares and toils. Its exhortations must be the guide of hand and foot and finger in the midst of all trial and temptation. Its words of comfort must be as lamps to burn and shine in sick-rooms and in the chambers of sorrow. Its visions of spiritual beauty must be translated into reality in conduct and character.

So, in all our life, the Sabbath's lessons must be lived out during the week; the patterns of heavenly things shown in the mount must be wrought into forms of reality and act and disposition and character. The love of God which so warms our hearts as we think of it must flow out in love to men. We must be Christians on Monday as well as on the Sabbath. Our religion must touch every part of our life and transform it all into the beauty of holiness.

VI.

COMPENSATION IN LIFE.

"For the rapture of love is linked with the pain or fear of loss,
And the hand that takes the crown must ache with many a cross;
Yet he who hath never a conflict hath never a victor's palm,
And only the toilers know the sweetness of rest and calm."

FRANCES RIDLEY HAVERGAL.

EVERY shadow has its light; every night has its morning; every pang of pain has its thrill of pleasure; every salt tear has its crystal beauty; every weakness has its element of strength; every loss has its gain. So all through life these balancings run.

He is not a thoughtful or reverent observer who has not been struck by this wonderful system of compensations found in all God's providences. Wherever we turn we can see it, if only we have eyes to see. It may be traced even in nature. Every hill or mountain has its corresponding valley. The disadvantages of any particular place are balanced by advantages of some kind. Asher's portion was hilly, but in the rugged hills there were minerals; the paths were rough and steep, but there was iron at hand with which to prepare shoes for the hard climbing. Marah's waters were bitter and unfit to drink, but close beside the fountain grew the tree to sweeten them. Summer's heat is hard to endure, but it woos from the earth ten thousand lovely beauties of verdure, foliage, flower and harvest. Autumn comes with its fading leaves, its perishing flowers, its dying life and its sadness, but it is the season of purple vintage, mellowing fruits and falling nuts, while the foliage in its very decay surpasses the glory of its freshest greenness. Winter has its short days, its snows and its piercing colds, but it brings its long nights, its social cheer, its crystal beauty, its merry sports, while beneath its fleecy blankets the roots of trees, grasses, grains and flowers are nourished. Spring has its rains, its melting snows, its cloudy skies, its impassable country-roads, but it has also its bursting buds, its return of birds, its warm breathings and all its prophecies of life and beauty.

In human life also we find the same law of compensation. Men's lots are not so unlike as we ofttimes think them to be. Every ill has somewhere a good to balance it, and every envied portion has something in it which detracts from its enjoyment. It makes a great difference from what point of view we look at life's experiences and circumstances. From one outlook only the attractive features are seen, while the drawbacks are concealed in the brightness. From another position only the unfavorable qualities appear, while the beauties are eclipsed in the shadows. There is a great difference also in people's eyes. Some see only the sternness and the blemishes, but surely they are wiser who see even the little bits of loveliness that gleam out always amid the sternness like beautiful vines and sweet flowers on the cold, bare mountain-crags.

There is never an inconvenience in life but has its compensating benefit, if only we have patience and faith enough to find it. The world is very large, with a great many people besides ourselves in it, and we must not expect all the compensation to come to us. Sometimes we may have to take a measure of discomfort that our neighbor may reap a blessing. The rain that hurts our grass may be a boon to his garden. The wind that impedes the speed of our boat may fill his sails. "It's an ill wind that blows nobody any good." Only selfishness can forget that there are people who live beyond the hill, and that our inconvenience may be their advantage.

Even in our prayers we need to remember that what we desire may come to us only at the loss or the harming of another. Thus we are trained to temper our cravings and moderate our asking for ourselves. One writes:

"What sorrow we should beckon unawares,
    What stinging-nettles in our path would grow,
If God should answer all our thoughtless prayers,
    Or bring to harvest the poor seed we sow!

"The storm for which you prayed, whose kindly shock
    Revived your fields and blessed the fainting air,
Drove a strong ship upon the cruel rock,
    And one I loved went down in shipwreck there.

"I ask for sunshine on my grapes to-day,
    You plead for rain to kiss your drooping flowers;
And thus within God's patient hand we lay
    These intricate cross-purposes of ours.

"I greeted with cold grace and doubting fears
    The guest who proved an angel at my side,
And I have shed more bitter, burning tears
    Because of hopes fulfilled than prayers denied.

"Then be not clamorous, O restless soul!
    But hold thy trust in God's eternal plan:
He views our life's dull weaving as a whole;
    Only its tangled threads are seen by man.

> "Dear Lord, vain repetitions are not meet
>   When we would bring our messages to thee;
> Help us to lay them at thy dear feet
>   In acquiescence, not garrulity."

There is ground of comfort, therefore, when our requests for ourselves are not granted, in the thought that blessing may have been given to some other one through the denying to us of our wishes. This ought to be to us an answer, for we are to love our neighbor as ourself.

But usually the compensation lies nearer home. The poor boy who has to work hard, and who lacks the comforts and the good times that are enjoyed by the rich man's son, finds balancing good in the rugged health, the habits of industry and the manliness and self-reliance that are the fruit of his daily toils, tasks and hardships. The man who labors all the day and is weary at nightfall has compensation in his relish for food and in the sweetness of his sleep. The poor man may have fewer comforts and greater privations, but he has none of the rich man's anxieties and cares. Lowly places in life may be less conspicuous and there may be smaller honor attached to them, but there is also less responsibility; for to whom much is given, of them also much is required. Besides, content is more likely to dwell in the quiet valley than on the mountain-top.

We may turn the lesson in other ways. If there is a steep hill to climb, the toil is repaid by the grander and wider view obtained from the summit. On the other hand, the quiet, lowly vales may seem very commonplace under the shadow of the great hills, but they have their own advantages. They are sheltered from the storms, and the soil in them, receiving the wash from the hills, is richer. Getting up toward the stars appears to be promotion, but it is getting up, also, amid the tempests. Advancement brings fresh honor, but it also lays upon the shoulders new cares and burdens. One night in the darkest period of our American civil war President Lincoln and a friend were standing at a window in the White House looking out at the driving storm. The friend made some remark concerning the sufferings of the soldiers in the camps on such a night. The President replied that there was not a soldier in any of the camps with whom he would not gladly exchange places.

In personal experiences the same balancing is found. Pain is hard to endure, but it has also its compensation, unless by our own impatience and unbelief we rob ourselves of the comfort which God always sends with it and in it. Pain is meant to purify and whiten. Those who wear the radiant garments in glory are they who have come up out of great tribulation. Thousands of sufferers have learned their richest and best life-lessons in sore trials. The fires are hot, but holiness comes out of the flames. The pruning is sharp and cuts to the heart, but more and better fruit is the result afterward. The earthly loss is sore, but there is rich spiritual gain that comes from it. On the briery rod lovely roses grow, and many of the sweetest blessings of life are gathered from amid grief's sharp thorns. An old poet wrote in quaint phrase:

"Venomous thorns, that are so sharp and keen,
  Bear flowers, we see, full fresh and fair of hue;
Poison is also put in medicine,
  And unto man his health doth oft renew.
The fire that all things eke consumeth clean
  May hurt and heal; then if that this be true,
I trust some time my harm may be my health,
Since every woe is joinèd with some wealth."

Sorrow comes, and sorrow is always bitter and hard to endure, but divine comfort comes with it, unless in our blindness we thrust the blessed angel from our door. It was the Master himself who said, "Blessed are they that mourn: for they shall be comforted." This beatitude can mean only that God's comfort is so rich an experience, so great a blessing, to those who receive it that it is well worth our while to mourn that we may get the comfort. Those who do not mourn, therefore, lose one of the richest, sweetest beatitudes of divine love. Night draws down over us with its darkness, and we dread its coming; but when it deepens above our heads and day fades out of the sky, ten thousand stars flash out. The glorious stars are rich compensation for the darkness. So it is when the night of sorrow approaches. We shudder at its coming on, but we pass into its shadows, and heavenly comforts which we had not seen before appear glowing in silvery splendor above our heads. In the bright summer days clouds gather and blot out the blue of the sky and fill the air with ominous gloom and with fierce lightnings and terrific thunder-peals, but out of the clouds rain pours down to refresh the thirsty earth and to give new life to the flowers and the plants. So it is, also, with the clouds of trial whose black folds ofttimes gather above us in our fair summer days of gladness: there is rich compensation in the blessings the heavy clouds bear to our lives.

There is a class of people in every community

who have bodily imperfections or maimings of some kind which ofttimes seem to be sore misfortunes. Sometimes it is lameness that prevents a man from joining in life's swift race with his fellows, or it is blindness which shuts out the glories of day and dooms a man to walk in darkness, or it is some bodily deformity which mars the beauty of the human form; or it may be only confirmed physical feebleness which makes one a lifelong invalid.

Is there any compensation for these misfortunes? No doubt there are possible compensations in every case. Byron with his hideous clubbed foot had a marvelous genius. It is well known that blindness is almost invariably alleviated by the wonderful acuteness of the other senses. The late Mr. Fawcett of England said once to a company of blind people, "Those only know who have felt it by their own experience the wonderful compensatory forces which nature supplies. Although I should be the last to underrate what is lost by those who cannot see with their eyes all the countless beauties of color and of form, the landscape bright with sunshine or silvered over in the moonlight calm, yet, in some manner too subtle for me to attempt to analyze, the mental effect of association is so great that I find that the greatest pleasure can be derived from scenes I cannot see. If I am out walking or riding, I should feel it a distinct loss if I were not told that there was a beautiful sunset. A great poet has said:

> 'There is a budding morrow in midnight,
> There is a triple sight in blindness keen.'"

No doubt every misfortune brings within reach some compensating advantage, although it may not always be possible to tell what it is. There is in every case at least the compensation of human love and sympathy. Dr. J. G. Holland has well said, "The mother of a poor misshapen idiotic boy will, though she have half a score of bright and beautiful children besides, entertain for him a peculiar affection. He may not be able in his feeble-mindedness to appreciate it, but her heart brims with tenderness for him; and if he be a sufferer, the softest pillow and the tenderest nursing will be his. A love will be bestowed upon him which gold could not buy, and which no beauty of person and no brilliancy of natural gifts could possibly awaken. It is thus with every case of defect or eccentricity of person. So sure as the mother of a child sees in that child's person any reason for the world to regard it with contempt or aversion, does she treat it with peculiar tenderness, as if she were commissioned by God—as, indeed, she is—to make up to it in the best coinage that which the world will certainly neglect to bestow."

The practical value of this study lies in the direction of contentment. Whatever may be our circumstances, there is in them a nice balancing of advantages and disadvantages which ought to keep us on the one hand from elation or pride, and on the other from undue depression or disheartenment. We need not envy those whose lot seems better than our own; for if we knew all their life, we should find amid the prosperities some drawback that in discomfort fully counterbalances that which seems to us so attractive and enviable. We ought not to grieve over the hardness or the trial in our own lot, for, whatever it is, it has some compensation that makes it a real—or, certainly, a possible—blessing.

So we get here a lesson of peace. Not accidental are the events which befall us or the circumstances by which our lives are borne along; all are directed by the hand of divine wisdom and love, and the good and the ill are so balanced that "all things work together for good to them that love

God." Every ill carries in its bosom a **compensating good**; every dark cloud has **its** lining **of** silver.

"Ah! if we knew it all, we should surely understand
  That the balance of sorrow and joy is held with an even hand,
  That the scale of success or loss shall never overflow,
  And that compensation is twined with the lot of high and low."

Thus, from whatever side **we** look **at life, we find this law of** compensation. **Toil is** hard, but toiling knits the thews of strength and toughens the fibres. Burdens are heavy, but life grows into calm power under the weight. Crosses bring pain, but they lift men up nearer to God. Duty is exacting and allows **no rest, but** faithfulness brings its blessed reward. There **is no loss** but wrapped **up in it is a** seed of gain; there is no darkness but **has its lamp** shining somewhere in its very **midst** to illumine it.

"No chilly snow **but** safe below
  A million buds are sleeping,
No wintry days but fair spring rays
  Are swiftly onward sweeping.

"No note **of** sorrow but shall melt
  In sweetest chord unguessed;
No labor all too pressing felt
  But ends in quiet rest."

Can it be but blind chance that produces all this marvelous result? Can it be only nature's working that so adjusts all the ten thousand wheels of life's intricate machinery that in their motions they evolve only harmonies in the end? Could any mere chance so set a good opposite every ill, a comfort over against every sorrow, a blessing to offset every trial? It would be no less incredible a thing if one were to assert that once a printer flung down a font of types and the letters accidentally so arranged themselves as to produce in perfect lines, paragraphs and pages the Gospel of St. John.

VII.

THE COST OF BEING A BLESSING.

"Say not, ''Twas all in vain—
 The anguish and the darkness and the strife:
Love thrown upon the waters comes again."
ANNA SHIPTON.

"Others shall
Take patience, labor, to their heart and hand
From thy hand and thy heart and thy brave cheer,
And God's grace fructify through thee to all."
E. B. BROWNING.

OUR preachers sometimes tell us, in urging us to live a useful life, that it costs but little to do good. In a sense this is true. Without large outlay of money and without great expenditure of strength one may do many helpful things and make one's life a rich blessing in the world; yet there is a deeper sense in which one cannot be a true blessing in this world save at much cost.

"What had she done?" asks one, in referring to a life which had filled a home with benedictions. "Absolutely nothing; but radiant smiles, beaming good-humor, the tact of divining what every one felt and every one wanted, told that she had got out of self and learned to think of others; so that at one time it showed itself in deprecating by sweet words the quarrel which lowering brows and raised tones already showed to be impending; at another, by soothing an invalid's pillow; at another, by soothing a sobbing child; at another, by humoring and softening a father who had returned weary and ill-tempered from the irritating cares of business. None but she saw those things; none but a loving heart could see them. That was the secret of her heavenly power. The one who will be found in trial capable of great acts of love is ever the one who is always doing considerate small ones."

Such ministries seem to cost nothing: they flow from lip and hand and heart quietly and naturally as if no effort were required to perform them. Yet the least of them is the fruit of self-denial and sacrifice. They cost heart's blood. No real good or blessing of any kind do we ever get that has not cost some other one a pang or a tear. Nor can we in our turn do good to others without cost. The life that is to be a beneficent one cannot be one of ease and selfish enjoyment. Even a grain of wheat must fall into the ground and die before it can yield any harvest. To become useful and helpful we must die to self and to personal ambitions and longings: "He that loveth his life shall lose it; and he that hateth his life in this world shall keep it unto life eternal."

We may have our choice. We may live for self, taking good care of our lives, not exposing them to danger, not making personal sacrifices, having a keen eye always for our own interests and advancement. By this plan of life we may come to old age hale and with our strength unabated. People may congratulate us on our well-preserved state, and we may have considerable pride in the outcome of our prudence and carefulness. There certainly seems to be something quite pleasant and attractive in such a life, yet really it is only the grain of wheat remaining safe and dry in the garner and kept from falling into the earth. It is well preserved, but there is no harvest from it. The life abides by itself alone, well enough kept, but with no increase. It has been no blessing to the world. It has wrought no ministry of love.

But there is another way to live. It is altogether to forget self—not to think of nor care for one's own life, but to throw it away in obedience to God and in the service of others. People will say we are foolish thus to waste our golden life, to wear ourselves out in toils that bring us no return, to make sacrifices for others who are not worthy. They sought to hold Jesus back from his cross. They said his life was too precious to be wasted in such a way—that it ought to be kept for crowning and for reigning among men. But we understand now that Jesus made no mistake when he chose the way of sacrifice. The grain of wheat let fall into the ground has yielded a most glorious harvest. Jesus has never been sorry for the choice he made; he has never regretted Calvary.

The heart of the lesson is, that we cannot be blessings in this world and at the same time take good care of our own lives. That which has cost us nothing is worth nothing to others. This principle applies in every life and in all spheres. All along the ages whatever is good and beautiful and worthy has been the fruit of suffering and pain. Civilization has advanced through wars, revolutions and failures, through the ruin, decay and overturning of empires and kingdoms. Every thoughtful reader of the world's history understands this. What Christian civilization is to-day it is as the harvest of long, sad centuries of weary struggle, toil and oppression. Earth's thrones of power are built on the wreck of hopes that have been crushed,

Every **advance worth recording** has been made through carnage and disaster. It seems that without shedding of blood there is not only no remission of sin, but no progress in life, no growth. Heaven's victorious throngs wearing white robes and waving branches of palm come up out of great tribulation. Even Jesus appears in glory as a Lamb that has been slain; his blessedness and his saving power are the fruit of suffering and wounding to death. We know, too, that all the joys and honors of redemption come from the Saviour's cross, and that personal holiness can **be** reached **only through** struggle, conflict and the crucifixion of self. **Thus** whatever is good in earth and in heaven is the outcome of pain, sacrifice and death.

This law of the cost of whatever is best—even of all that is truly useful—in life finds illustration at every **point. We** cannot live a day but something must die to be food for the sustaining of our life. We cannot **be** warmed in winter but some miner must crouch **and** toil in darkness to provide **fuel** for our fires. We cannot be clothed but worms must weave their **own** lives into silk threads or sheep must shiver in the chill air that their fleeces may cover us. The gems and the jewels which the women wear, **and** which they prize so highly, **are** brought to them through the anguish and the peril of the poor wretches that hunt and dive for them, and the furs that we wrap about us in winter cost the lives of the creatures which first wore them, and which have to die to provide the warmth and the comfort for us. The child lives through the mother's pangs and anguish. We cannot even pray but pierced hands must be reached down to lift up to heaven our sighs and cries, and then held up in continual intercession to press our pleas before God. Divine mercy can come to us only through the blood of the Lamb.

It is doubtful whether in the realm of spiritual influence any blessing of real value ever comes to us from another which has not received its baptism of pains and tears. That which has cost nothing in the heart of him who gives it is not likely to be of great use to him who receives it. The true poets must always learn in suffering what they teach in song. The life-story told in the following lines is not exceptional:

> "The poet dipped his pen and drew
>   His vivid pictures phrase by phrase—
> Of skies and misty mountains blue,
>   Of starry nights and shimmering days.
> Men said, 'He breedeth fancies pure;
> His touch is facile, swift and sure.'

"The poet's friend was stricken sore;
  In tender tears the pen he dipped,
And breathed his gentle sorrow o'er,
  And traced the sympathetic script.
Men said, 'His heart is kind and true;
The laurel yet shall **be his due.**'

"The poet's child has waxen hands
  That hold Death's heavy-scented rose;
She drifts to the dim shadow-lands,
  And draws his wild soul as she goes.

    *   *   *   *   *

He dipped his pen in his heart's wound,
And sobbing wrote, and thus was crowned."

The story of all the world's best thoughts is the same. **The** things in men's writings that really and deeply help us they have learned in pain **and** anguish, in sore mental conflicts or in suffering. The words of the preacher, however eloquently and fluently uttered, which he has not himself **been** taught in experiences of struggle, may please the ear and charm the fancy, but they do not greatly help or bless others. **We all** know that the most effective oratory is **not** that which flows without effort from **the** lips **of** the speaker, but that which in the knit brow, the glowing eye and the trembling voice tells of strong feeling and of cost of **life.** All great thoughts are the fruit of deep pondering, **and** ofttimes of suffering and struggle.

"Wherever a great thought is born," said one who knew by bitter experience, "there always is Gethsemane."

An English preacher wrote to one who had thanked him for help received from his sermons: "That a ministry in which words and truth—if truth come, wrung out of mental pain and inward struggle—should now and then touch a corresponding chord in minds with which, from invincible and almost incredible shyness, I rarely come in personal contact, is not so surprising; for I suppose the grand principle is the universal one: we can heal one another only with blood." He meant that the lessons alone which have cost us pain, which we have learned in struggle, which have been born out of anguish of heart, will heal and really bless others. It is only when we have passed through the bitterness of temptation, wrestling with evil and sore beset ourselves, victorious only through the grace of Christ, that we are ready to be helpers of others in temptation. It is only when we have known sorrow, when the chords of our love have been swept by it and when we have been comforted by divine grace and helped to endure, that we are fitted to become comforters of others in their sorrow.

This law prevails, therefore, in all life. We yield blessing only through dying. There is a Chinese legend of a potter who sought for years and years to put a certain tint on the vases he made, but all his efforts failed. At last, discouraged and in despair, he threw himself into his furnace, and his body was consumed in the fire; then when the vases were taken out, they bore the exquisite color he had striven so long in vain to produce. The legend illustrates the truth that we can do our noblest and best work only at cost of self. The alabaster box must be broken before its odors can flow out. Christ lifted up and saved the world, not by an easy, pleasant, successful life in it, but by suffering and dying in it and for it. And we can never bless the world merely by having a good time in it, but only by giving our lives for it.

Work for others that costs nothing is scarcely worth doing. At least, it takes heart's blood to heal hearts. Too many of us are ready to work for Christ and do good to our fellow-men only so long as it is easy and requires no sacrifice or self-denial; but if we stop there, we stop just where our service is likely to become of use. This saving of life proves, in the end, the losing of it. It is they who sow in tears who shall reap in joy. It is he that goeth forth and weepeth, bearing precious seed, that shall come again with rejoicing, bringing his sheaves with him. We may take easy work if we will—work that costs us nothing, that involves no pain or self-denial—but we must not then be surprised if our hands are empty in the great harvest-time.

VIII.

LIFE AS A LADDER.

"Beauty and truth, and all that these contain,
    Drop not like ripened fruit about our feet:
We climb to them through years of sweat and pain."

IT was a good while ago that a young man sleeping one night in the open air in a very desolate place had a wonderful vision of a ladder which started close beside him and sprang up into the very glory of heaven. The vision was meant to show him in heavenly picture what were his life's possibilities. The way lay open clear up to God; he could have communication with heaven now and always. Then the ladder visioned a path which his feet might tread, up and up, step by step, ever rising higher, until at the last he should be in the midst of heaven's glory.

We may say, too, without any straining of exegesis, without reading any fanciful interpretations into Scripture narrative, that the bright ladder was a picture of the Christ. Did not Jesus himself say, with this old-time vision in his mind, "Ye shall see heaven open, and the angels of God ascending and descending upon the Son of man"? As down to Jacob in his sinfulness came the ladder, so down into this lost world came the Saviour. The ladder reached from earth to heaven. See a picture of Christ's double nature: the Incarnation was the letting of the ladder down until it touched the lowest depths of human need; at the same time, our Lord's divinity reached up into heaven's blue, above the tallest mountains, above the shining stars, into the midst of the glory of God.

A ladder is a way for feet to climb; Christ is the way by which the worst sinners may go up out of their sins into the purity and blessedness of heaven. Homely though the figure of the ladder may be, it has many striking and instructive suggestions.

The ladder's foot rested on the ground; our lives start on the earth, ofttimes very low down, in the common dust. We do not begin our career as radiant angels, but as fallen mortals. We are all alike in this; the holiest saints began as sinners. He who would go up a ladder must first put his foot on the lowest round. We cannot start in Christian life at the top, but must begin at the bottom and climb up. He who would become a great scholar must first hold in his hand and diligently con the primer and the spelling-book; he who would rise to Christlikeness must begin with the simplest duties and obediences.

This ladder did not lie along the level plain, but rose upward until its top rested at the feet of God. Thus the path of every true life leads upward and ends in heaven. It is thus that the Scriptures always paint the way of Christian faith. "Whom he did foreknow, he also did predestinate to be conformed to the image of his Son." In God's first purpose of salvation for a sinner he has in mind the sinner's final transformation into the likeness of Christ. "It doth not yet appear what we shall be: but we know that, when he shall appear, we shall be like him." Whatever mystery may lie about the future state, this one thing is clear and sure—that every one who believes on Christ shall dwell with him and shall bear his image. The ladder of faith leads upward into the heavenly glory.

A ladder is climbed step by step; no one leaps to the top. No one rises to sainthood at a bound; slowly, step by step, we must rise in the heavenward way. No one gets the victory once for all over his sins and his faults. It is a struggle of long years, of the whole of life, and every day must have its own victories if we are ever to be crowned. Many people are discouraged because they seem never to get any nearer the end of their struggle; it is just as hard to be good and true this year as it was last year. This vision of life as a ladder shows that we may not expect to get beyond conflict and effort until our feet stand in heaven. A ladder is never easy to ascend; it is always toilsome work to go up its rounds. Railroad-tracks suggest speed and ease, but a ladder suggests slow and painful progress. We rise upward in spiritual life, not at railway speed, nor even at the racer's rate of progress, but slowly, as men go up a ladder.

Yet we may turn the lesson the other way: men do not fly up ladders, yet they go up step by step, continually rising. We certainly ought always to be making some progress in Christian life as the years go on. Each day should show at least a little advance in holiness, some new conquest over the evil that is in us, some wrong habit or some besetting sin gotten a little more under our feet. We ought always to be climbing upward, though it be but slowly. We ought never to stand still on the ladder.

The figure suggests, again, that we must do the

climbing ourselves. A ladder does not carry any one up: it is but a way of ascent provided for one who is willing to climb. God has made a way of salvation for us, but we must go in the way. He has let down the ladder and it springs from our feet up to the foot of heaven's throne, but we must climb its rounds; God will never carry us up. He helps us on the way—there were angels on the radiant stairway of Jacob—but we can never get upward one step without our own exertion. We are bidden to work out our own salvation, although we are assured that God works in us both to will and to do. He puts the good desires and impulses in our hearts, and then gives us the grace to work them out in life. It is God that cleanses us, but we must wash in the cleansing stream; God bears us to heaven, but our feet must do the climbing. Dr. J. G. Holland's lines are suggestive:

"Heaven is not reached by a single bound,
　But we build the ladder by which we rise
　From the lowly earth to the vaulted skies,
And we mount to its summit round by round.

"We rise by the things that are under our feet—
　By what we have mastered of good or gain,
　By the pride deposed and the passion slain,
And the vanquished ills that we hourly meet."

Every true life should thus be a perpetual climbing upward. We should put our faults under our feet and make them steps on which to lift ourselves daily a little higher. Longfellow in his "Ladder of St. Augustine" puts this thought in a striking way:

> "St. Augustine! well hast thou said
>   That of our vices we can frame
> A ladder, if we will but tread
>   Beneath our feet each deed of shame.
>
> "All common things, each day's events
>   That with the hour begin and end,
> Our pleasures and our discontents,
>   Are rounds by which we may ascend.
>
> * * * * *
>
> "Standing on what too long we bore
>   With shoulders bent and downcast eyes,
> We may discern—unseen before—
>   A path to higher destinies;
>
> "Nor deem the irrevocable past
>   As wholly wasted, wholly vain,
> If, rising on its wrecks, at last
>   To something nobler we attain."

We have here the key to all growth of character. We can rise only by continual self-conquests. We must make stepping-stones of our dead selves. Every fault we overcome lifts us a little higher. All low desires, all bad habits, all longings for ignoble things, that we vanquish and trample down, become ladder-rounds **on** which we climb **upward** out of earthliness and sinfulness into purer and Christlier being. **There** really is no other way by which we can rise upward. **If** we are not living victoriously these little common days, we surely are **not** making any progress. Only those **who** climb **are** mounting toward the stars. Heaven itself **at last,** and the heavenly life here on the earth, are **for those only** who overcome.

There **is another** suggestion **in** the figure: the **ladder which** began **on** the earth and pressed upward step by step reached **to the very feet of** God. It did not come to an end at the top of one of earth's high mountains. **God's way** of salvation **is not** partial, does not leave any climber halfway to glory, but conducts every **true** believer **to the gates of pearl.** The true Christian life is persistent **and** persevering; it endures unto the end. But we **must notice** that **it is** ladder all the way; it never **becomes a** plain, smooth, **flower-lined** or descending path. So long **as we** stay **in** this world we shall have to keep on climbing slowly, painfully, upward. A really true and earnest Christian life never gets **very** easy; the easy way of life does not **lead upward. If** we want just to have a good, pleasant time in this world, we may have it, but there will be no progress in it. It may be less difficult to live right after one has been living thus for a time, but the ladder never becomes a bit of level grass-sward. Every step of the heavenly way is uphill, and steep at that. Heaven always keeps above us, no matter how far we climb toward it. We never in this world get to a point where we may regard ourselves as having reached life's goal, as having attained the loftiest height within our reach; there are always other rounds of the ladder to climb. The noblest life ever lived on earth but began here its growth and attainment. Mozart, just before his death, said, "Now I begin to see what might be done in music." That is all the saintliest man ever learns in this world about living: he just begins to see what might be done in living. It is a comfort to know that that really is the whole of our earthly mission —just to learn how to live, and that the true living is to be beyond this world.

This wonderful vision-ladder was radiant with angels; we are not alone in our toilsome climbing. We have the companionship and ministry of strong friends whom we have never seen. Besides, the going up and coming down of these celestial messengers told of communication never interrupted between God and those who are climbing up the steep way. There is never a moment nor any experience in the life of a true Christian from which a message may not instantly be sent up to God, and back to which help may not instantly come. God is not off in heaven merely, at the top of the long, steep life-ladder, looking down upon us as we struggle upward in pain and tears. As we listen we hear him speak to the sad, weary man who lies there at the foot of the stairway, and he says, "Behold, I am with thee, and will keep thee in all places whither thou goest; . . . I will not leave thee." Not angel companionship alone, precious as that is, is promised, but divine companionship also, every step of the toilsome way until we get home. It is never impossible, therefore, for any one to mount the ladder to the very summit; with God's strong, loving help, the weakest need never faint nor fail.

IX.

SEEDS OF LIGHT.

"'Wouldst thou,' so the helmsman answered,
'Learn the secret of the sea?
Only those who brave its dangers
Comprehend its mystery.'"
LONGFELLOW.

"For meek obedience, too, is light,
And following that is finding Him."
LOWELL.

THE figure of the seed is very common in the Scriptures. All natural life begins in germs and develops into fullness of form and strength. The same law prevails in the spiritual world. The kingdom of heaven begins in a heart as a very little seed and grows until it fills all the life. Every word of God is a seed which encloses a living germ; plant it in the soil of faith and prayer, and it will grow.

There is one passage, however, in which the figure of the seed is very striking: "Light is sown for the righteous, and gladness for the upright in heart." "Light" stands for all spiritual blessing, and the thought is that our blessings are sown for us just as wheat-grains and flower-seeds are sown, and that we gather the harvest from this sowing as we pluck flowers from garden or wildwood or reap the wheat from the fields. God gives us our blessings not full-formed, but as seeds.

We may think of the divine sowing of the light we are now harvesting. We may say that before the world began God sowed seeds of light in his thoughts and purposes of redemption. There are trees on the earth which are many centuries old; one who sits in their shadow is lost in thought as he tries to think of the day when the seeds were dropped from which these ancient trees sprang. But the blessings of divine life in whose shade we sit these days in our homes and sanctuaries are older than the hoary mountains; they were thoughts and purposes of love in the heart of God in the immeasurable past, and are but growing to ripeness in these later days.

Then we may say that our blessed Lord sowed seeds of light for us in his incarnation, in his obedience, in his sufferings and in his atoning death. The tears that fell at Bethany and again on Olive's brow, the blood-drops of anguish that stained the dewy grass in Gethsemane and those other life-drops that trickled down from the cross on Golgotha,—these were all seeds of light sown to yield peace, joy, comfort and life to human souls along these centuries of Christian faith. Who can ever count up the blessings that the world has reaped from Christ's sowing?

Then we may say that God has sown light for us in his holy promises. All divine words are seeds; wherever they fall, beauty springs up. Deserts are made to blossom as the rose wherever the sower goes forth to sow. The promises were spoken ages since and put down in the inspired book and have been preserved, and now in these late times they bring cheer and hope to weary men who without them would perish in the darkness.

But there are more practical uses of the figure. A seed is a germ. When, therefore, we say that God has sown the light for us, we mean that he gives us our blessings in germ, not in full form— that they come to us, not developed into completeness of beauty, but as seeds which we must plant, waiting, sometimes waiting long, for them to grow into loveliness. A seed does not disclose all the beauty of the life that is folded up within it. We see only a little brown and unsightly hull which gives no prophecy of anything so beautiful as

springs from it when it has been planted. **These facts in** nature have their analogies in the seeds of spiritual blessing which God sows for us. The blessing does not appear; what does appear is often unlovely in its form, giving in itself no promise of good. Yet it is a seed carrying in it the potency of life and the possibilities of great blessing.

For example, every duty that comes to our hand in the common days is a seed of light which God **has** sown for us. Some seeds are dark and rough **as we look** upon them; **so** there are duties that have in them no promise of joy or pleasure as they first present themselves to us. They look hard and repulsive, and we shrink from doing them, **but** every one knows that there is in the faithful doing of every duty a strange secret of joy; and the harder the duty, the fuller and the richer is the sense of gladness that follows its performance.

> "God's angels drop like grains of gold
>   Our duties 'midst life's shining sands,
> And from them, one by one, we mould
>   **Our** own bright crown with patient hands.
> From dust and dross we gather them;
>   **We toil** and stoop **for** love's sweet sake
>   To **find** each worthy act a gem
>   In glory's kingly diadem
> Which we may daily richer make."

Thus every duty is a seed of light. To evade it or to neglect it is to miss a blessing; to do it is to have the seed burst into beauty in the heart of the doer. We need to learn the lesson. We are continually coming up to stern and severe things in our life's path, and ofttimes we are tempted to decline doing them because they appear hard and costly. If we yield to such temptations, we shall reap no joy from God's sowing of light for us; but if we take up the hard task, whatever it is, and do it, we shall always find blessing.

One of our Lord's own words will help us here. When, at the well of Jacob, his disciples pressed him to eat, knowing that a little while before he had been weary and hungry, his answer was, "I have meat to eat that ye know not of."—"Hath any man brought him aught to eat?" they inquired. Then Jesus answered, "My meat is to do the will of Him that sent me, and to finish his work." That is, he took up the duties that came to him hour by hour, hard as they might be, and in doing them found bread for his hunger. These duties, so to speak, were like nuts, hard and with rough, prickly hull, which yet, when broken open, yield delicious meat. There is always in every doing of God's will a secret gladness that feeds the soul. God's commandments ever enfold seeds of blessing whose ripened fruit can never become ours unless we obey the divine words. Says the old Hebrew Psalmist,

"The law of the Lord is perfect, restoring the soul;
The testimony of the Lord is sure, making wise the simple;
The precepts of the Lord are right, rejoicing the heart;
The commandment of the Lord is pure, enlightening the eyes;
The fear of the Lord is clean, enduring for ever;
The judgments of the Lord are true, and righteous altogether.
More to be desired are they than gold, yea, than much fine gold;
Sweeter also than honey and the honeycomb.
Moreover by them is thy servant warned;
In keeping of them is there great reward."

In all these expressions the blessing appears wrapped up in the divine will. We must keep the law, and it will restore our soul; we must observe the precepts, and they will rejoice our heart; we must obey the commandment, and it will enlighten our eyes; we must eat the honey to taste its sweetness; we must keep the statutes to get their great reward. Thus God has sown seeds of light all along our path, in all the tasks and duties of our common days; if we will be obedient always, our lives shall be ever full of blessings.

The providences that God sends us are likewise

seeds of light. They are *seeds* of light, for the light is not always manifest in them as at first they appear to our eyes. Ofttimes they have a dark and unattractive aspect; they come in the form of trials, losses, disappointments, pains.

Here is a lump of black coal which the miner brings up from the depths of the earth. He tells you to take it into your house and it will fill your apartment with light; but you shrink from touching it, and say, "Surely there is no light in that? See! it only blackens my fingers. It can shed no beams of light in my room." Yet that lump of coal is indeed a seed of light. The man of science takes it and puts it in his retort, and your chamber is made bright as day by its unimprisoned beams.

Many of the providences that God sends to us are in like manner repulsive in their form. We shrink from them. "There surely can be no hidden light in this trial," we say. "There can be no concealed gladness in this grief or pain." Yet it is just as in the lump of coal: there is a seed of light folded up and hidden away in the hard experience. There is a word in the Epistle to the Hebrews which carries the same thought: "No chastening for the present seemeth to be joyous, but grievous; nevertheless, afterward it yieldeth

7

the peaceable fruit of righteousness unto them which are exercised thereby." At first there is no fruit, only a seed, and that is dark, unattractive —not joyous, but grievous. Then afterward, at the time of ripening, the fruit comes, beautiful, luscious —the peaceable fruit of righteousness.

> "Within this leaf, to every eye
> So little worth, doth hidden lie
> Most rare and subtile fragrancy.
> Wouldst thou its secret strength unbind?
> Crush it, and thou shalt perfume find
> Sweet as Arabia's spicy wind.
>
> "In this dull stone, so poor, and bare
> Of shape or lustre, patient care
> Will find for thee a jewel rare;
> But first must skillful hands essay,
> With file and flint, to clear away
> The film which hides its fire from day.
>
> "This leaf? this stone? It is thy heart.
> It must be crushed by pain and smart,
> It must be cleansed by sorrow's art,
> Ere it will yield a fragrance sweet,
> Ere it will shine a jewel meet
> To lay before thy dear Lord's feet."

The lesson is plain: every dark providence that comes to us is a seed of light. The light is concealed in the rough covering; but if we take the seed and plant it in the furrow gashed in our heart by the pain, it will in due time yield its blessed fruit of light. It requires time to get the plant of beauty from the seed; the seed must lie in the ground and die that the living germ enfolded in the husk may shoot up. So we have to wait a while —sometimes a long while—to get the blessing out of the sorrow or the pain that God gives to us. We must give the seed time to grow. Yet we need faith and patience to get the rich blessing. Not to be able to accept the bitterness of the seed is to miss the sweetness of the ripened fruit. No doubt many persons fail of the highest and best blessings of life because they cannot take the pain or the severity in which the blessings are wrapped.

Every cross which we are called to take up is also a seed of light. We are strongly tempted in these luxurious days to seek out for ourselves easy ways of life and to evade those that are hard. Naturally, we do not like to bear heavy burdens, to perform difficult tasks, to make self-denials and sacrifices. We prefer to be indolent. Not many people die of overwork; far more die of *ennui*. Souls as well as bodies are withered and shriveled by self-indulgence.

When we are having great worldly prosperity, getting on easily, without much trial or struggle, we think we are enjoying God's special favor and are being peculiarly blessed by him; but when times get harder, when there is more conflict, when there **are** fewer pleasant things, we think we are not having so much divine **favor as** formerly. But we are wrong in inferring this. It is a mis**taken** thought that God sows life's best blessings thickest amid the flowers of earth's gardens; really, they lie most plentifully on the bare fields of **toil and hardship.** Luxury has not in it half so many germs and possibilities of real good **as** are found along **the** sterner paths **of** life. The poor man's boy envies the rich man's **son** because the latter does **not** need **to do** anything or to exert himself **to** get started **in** life; the poor boy wishes his lot **were** the same, and laments the hardness of **the circum**stances in which he is doomed to toil and struggle. The angel that bends over the boy's head in guar**dian care** sees the seeds of a great harvest of blessing in the very things the boy bewails as discouragements and hardnesses. The need for exertion, self-denial and endurance, **for doing** without many things which he craves, and working early and late to get the **bare** necessities **of** existence, builds up in **him** a strong, self-reliant **manhood.** Idleness anywhere and always is a curse and brings a **curse** upon itself, while work anywhere and always is a blessing and brings blessing upon itself.

> "Get leave to work
> In this world: 'tis the best you get at all:
> For God, in cursing, gives us better gifts
> Than man in benediction. God says, 'Sweat
> For foreheads;' men say, 'Crowns;' and so we are crowned—
> Ay, gashed by some tormenting circle of steel
> Which snaps with a secret spring. Get work! get work!
> Be sure 'tis better than what you work to get."

Of course toil and hardship are not easy, nor is it easy to take up the cross and carry it; but if we are wise, it is not ease that we are seeking, but good—growth, blessing, character, more life. It was not easy for Jesus to go forward to his cross seeing it ever in plain view, yet we remember with what horror he looked upon the thought of turning away from it when a disciple sought to dissuade him from going on to meet it. We are told, also, that he endured the cross, despising the shame, for the joy that was set before him. To his eye the cross was a seed of light; the light—what wondrous light it was!—was wrapped up in the black folds. He took up the seed of ignominy and shame and woe, and out of it burst all the glorious blessings of human redemption.

So it is in all life, in the largest and the humblest

and in the smallest and the greatest things: **God wraps up** his best things in dark coverings, in husks that repel **us by their** sharpness **and their** bitterness. The law of all true living is toil, endurance, pain, sacrifice. Nothing of much worth can be gotten without cost. **An** easy life has but small outcome. **We** shrink from things that **are** hard, but really all calls to stern and severe duties are seeds of light; they are calls to accept divine **gifts of inestimable worth.** The hard tasks carry within themselves germs of **good** and blessing. **Crosses blossom into** crowns. All calls to self-denials are invitations to fuller life, to nobler manhood. If we accept them **in** quiet faith and with heroic courage, we shall gather blessings into our bosom in the harvest-time.

> "If none were sick and none were sad,
>   What service could we render?
> I think if we were always glad
>   We scarcely could be tender.
> Did our beloved never need
>   Our patient ministration,
> Earth would grow cold, and miss indeed
>   Its sweetest consolation.
> If sorrow never claimed our heart
>   And **every** wish **were** granted,
> Patience would die and hope depart—
>   Life would be disenchanted."

These are illustrations enough to make clear the principle. We are coming up to the seeds of light continually as we go on over life's hard paths. They may not lie like pearls of dew on leaf and flower, nor like diamonds blazing out their light; ofttimes they are rough, with prickly burrs which it hurts our hands to take up; but afterward, when they have had time to grow, the fruit reveals itself. Every heavenly impulse obeyed lights in our hearts a lamp whose beam at length flames out. Every hard duty accepted and performed yields its secret of joy; every sacrifice endured for Christ's sake brings its blessing.

But if we will not accept the rough seeds, we never can have the ripe fruit; hence only heroic souls can get the best things of life. Easy faith receives but small reward; its timid vessels venture not beyond sight of land. Only bold faith discovers new worlds. Only to those who overcome are the Apocalyptic blessings promised. The joys of victory none can taste but those who pass through the battle.

X.

LOOKING AT THE RIGHT SIDE.

"Now in the sunset glow I stand so near
　The hills of light that all the past grows clear;
　Even griefs, transfigured in this softer ray,
　Take on new forms and shine above my way.
　With dawning triumph in the words I read,
　'He taketh from us nothing that we need.'"

FRANCES L. MACE.

VERY much heart-pain is caused by looking at the wrong side of providences. If we could only see the strange things of our lives in their true light, perplexity would vanish and the darkest experiences would be brightened as night is brightened by the shining stars.

Late on a summer afternoon rain began to fall. For half an hour it fell in gentle shower. All the while the sky in the low west was cloudless, and the sun, near his setting, shone in undimmed radiance. Through the falling shower his beams poured, making a scene of wonderful beauty. The crystal raindrops looked like diamonds as the sun's rays touched them, and the whole air seemed full of brilliant gems. Arching the eastern horizon a wondrous rainbow appeared, all its colors dazzling in their bright beauty. So it is to the eye of Christian faith when the clouds of trial gather overhead and the rain falls: it is still clear where the Father looks down upon his children. No clouds cover his face; the beams of his love stream through the falling shower; every teardrop becomes a precious gem and the rainbow of peace glows upon the clouds. The Christian needs only to behold his sorrow in the true light to see it thus transfigured.

> "Be still, sad heart, and cease repining:
> Behind the clouds is the sun still shining.
> Thy fate is the common fate of all:
> Into each life some rain must fall,
>   Some days must be dark and dreary."

One Christmas a friend sent the poet Whittier a gentian-flower pressed between two pieces of glass. On one side the appearance was without beauty— only an indistinct, blurred mass of something held beneath the pane—but on the other side the full exquisite beauty of the flower appeared delicately outlined under the glass. The poet hung the token on his window, turning the lovely side inward. Those who passed by without, looking up, marked only a "gray disc of clouded glass," seeing no beauty, perchance wondering that the poet would cherish anything so void of grace; but he, sitting within, looked at the token, **and** saw outlined against the winter **sky** all the exquisite loveliness of the flower.

> "They cannot from their outlook see
> The perfect grace it has for me;
> For there the flower whose fringes through
> The frosty breath of autumn blew
> Turns from without its face of bloom
> To the warm tropic of my room,
> **As fair** as when beside its brook
> **The hue** of bending skies it took.
>
> "**But** deeper meanings come **to me,**
> My half-immortal flower, from thee:
> Man judges from a partial view;
> None ever yet his brother knew.
> The eternal Eye that sees the whole
> May better read the darkened soul,
> And find, to outward sense denied,
> The flower upon its inmost side."

There is a side of perfect beauty in every providence of Christian life, and there is also a side that is dark, blurred, or even repellent. To those who look at the providence **from** within, sitting in **the** chamber of faith and peace, it appears in all **the** colors of heaven; **but** to those who stand outside, **in the** winter's cold, and look at it, it appears without one line of loveliness. Only those who behold God as their Father see the beauty in his providences.

Our Lord in his parable of the Vine and its Branches tells us two things which ought to help in the interpreting of life's trials. He says that the Father is the husbandman, and also that it is the fruitful branches, and not the unfruitful, that the husbandman prunes. Afflictions are never in themselves joyous or pleasant. We cannot welcome them into our lives in the same way that we welcome experiences of gladness; they always give pain, and we cannot enjoy pain. Many of them cut deeply and sorely into our lives. Sometimes our best-beloved friends are taken away from us, and our hearts are left bleeding as a vine bleeds when a green branch is cut from it. Sometimes it is loss of property or of money that tries us, or it may be in sickness or personal suffering that the chastening consists. In whatever form it comes, the experience is painful. It cannot be otherwise.

Here it is that Christian faith comes in, putting such interpretation and explanation upon the painful things that we may be ready to accept them with confidence, even with rejoicing. The assurance which our Lord gives that the Father is the husbandman, if we can but receive it in simplicity, at once puts a gracious and loving aspect on whatever sufferings we are called to endure. Our Father is the husbandman; we are branches under his care. He watches over our lives. The afflictions which cut into our very souls, the taking from us of objects that are dear to us, as when the gardener with his sharp knife removes luxuriant branches from the vine, are our Father's prunings. No hand but his ever holds the knife. We are sure, then, that there is never any careless cutting, any unwise or mistaken pruning, any needless removing of rich branches or growths.

We really need to go no farther than this. A strong, abiding confidence that all the trials, sorrows and losses of our lives are parts of our Father's husbandry ought to silence every question, quiet every fear and give peace and restful assurance to our hearts in all their pain. We cannot know the reason for the painful strokes, but we know that He who holds the pruning-knife is our Father. That ought always to be enough to know.

The other thought in the Lord's parable is scarcely less full of comfort to a Christian. He says it is the fruitful branches that the Father prunes: "Every branch that beareth fruit he purgeth."

Afflictions are not, then, a mark of God's anger or disapproval; rather, they are a mark of his favor. They show that the branches into which he cuts, from which he trims away the luxuriant growths, are fruit-bearing already. He does not prune the fruitless branches: he cuts them off altogether as useless, as mere cumberers, absorbing life and yielding nothing of blessing or good. There is no place in the divine kingdom for uselessness. God may let these barren branches alone for a while—they may grow undisturbed even until death before they are actually cut off—but the Father does not take the trouble to prune them, because it would do no good. They are in Christ only in appearance, not really, and have no true life in them. The wisest and most skillful pruning will never make fruitful a lifeless tree or vine.

Some good Christian people have the impression that their many troubles indicate that God does not love them—that they cannot be true Christians, or they would not be so chastened. This word of Christ shows how mistaken they are. The much chastening shows that the Father is pruning his fruitful branch to make it more fruitful: "Whom the Lord loveth he chasteneth." Long ago the writer of one of the Psalms passed through an experience of perplexity when he saw how much less trouble men of the world had than he had, though he was faithfully trying to serve God. The record of his experience is valuable to us:

> "But as for me, my feet were almost gone;
> My steps had wellnigh slipped.
> For I was envious at the arrogant,
> When I saw the prosperity of the wicked.
> For there are no bands in their death;
> But their strength is firm.
> They are not in trouble as other men;
> Neither are they plagued like other men."

But the writer passes on to note the result of this absence of trouble or pruning:

> "Therefore, pride is as a chain about their neck;
> Violence covereth them as a garment.
> Their eyes stand out with fatness:
> They have more than heart could wish,
> They scoff, and in wickedness utter oppression;
> They speak loftily.
>   *   *   *   *   *   *
> Behold, these are the wicked;
> And, being alway at ease, they increase in riches."

Then there rises up before the Psalmist the contrasted picture of his own life, and the question flashes, "Does it profit to be good?"

> "Surely in vain have I cleansed my heart,
> And washed my hands in innocency;

> For all the day long have I been plagued,
> And chastened every morning."

A little later, however, we hear the solution of the strange perplexity:

> "When I thought how I might know this,
> It was too painful for me;
> Until I went into the sanctuary of God,
> And considered their latter end.
> Surely thou settest them in slippery places;
> Thou casteth them down to destruction.
> How are they become a desolation in a moment!
> They are utterly consumed with terrors."

That one escapes the Father's prunings is not, therefore, a mark of peculiar divine love and favor. It is the fruitless branch that is never pruned; the fruitful branch is pruned, and pruned —not by one without skill, not by an enemy, but by the wise Father. Thus we see how we may even rejoice in our trials and afflictions. They are tokens that God loves us—that we are already blessed by him in spiritual fruiting—and they remind us that it is because God would lead us to be yet greater blessings by making us still more fruitful that he sends the trials.

We get from our Lord's parable also another word of interpretation; we learn that our Father has a definite object in view in all his prunings:

"**Every** branch that beareth fruit he **purgeth [or pruneth] it, that it** may bring forth more fruit." One who was altogether ignorant of the art of pruning and its purpose, who should see a man with a sharp knife cutting off branch after branch of a luxuriant vine, would at first suppose that the pruner was ruining the vine. So at the time it seems, but by and by it appears that the prunings have made **the** vine more fruitful. In the season of vintage the grapes are more luscious, with a richer flavor in **them, because** of **the** cutting away of the superfluous branches. In like manner, if an angel who **had never** witnessed anything **of** human suffering, and who knew nothing of its object, were to see the Father causing pain and affliction to his children, it would seem to him that these experiences could be only destructive of happiness and blessing ; but if the angel were to follow those chastened lives on to the end, he would see untold blessing coming out of the chastenings. The Father was but pruning the branches that they might bear more and better fruit:

> "Now the pruning, sharp, unsparing,
>   Scattered blossom, bleeding shoot;
> Afterward the plenteous bearing
>   Of the Master's pleasant fruit."

In one of his Psalms, David says, "I had fainted,

unless I had believed to see the goodness of the Lord, in the land of the living." He had been passing through many and sore troubles, and so great were his trials that he would have sunk into utter darkness and despair but for his faith in a goodness which he could not see. Unless he had *believed* to see the goodness he would have been overwhelmed. There are many times when we can readily discern the divine goodness in our lives—it is manifest all about us, in prosperities and favors which make us glad—but there come other times when the goodness cannot be seen. The home circle is broken; loved ones are taken from us; property melts away; friends fail; health is shattered. The goodness cannot be seen.

Then is the time for Christian faith. We should believe in the goodness we cannot see. We are sure that the goodness is there. God does not send us two classes of providences—one good, and one evil. All are good. Affliction is God's goodness in the seed. It takes time for a seed to grow and to develop into fruitfulness. Many of the best things of our lives come to us first as pain, suffering, earthly loss or disappointment—black seeds, without beauty—but afterward they grow into the rich fruits of righteousness.

God's love toward his children **never intermits.** His will is always mercy and love. Ofttimes **there is more divine blessing** in the things we regard as **evil** than in those we consider good. Pain may be better for us to-morrow than pleasure. Loss may have for us greater enriching than gain. Sorrow **may** work for us better service than joy in the fashioning of Christ's image on our hearts. Misfortune, as we interpret the experience, may bring us in**finitely more** blessing than **the** events we **write** down as fortunate. Our wrecks of earthly hopes **may be in reality** the disclosing to us of rich **spiritual** possessions unseen before.

In one of our light, thoughtless, superficial words **we say,** "Seeing is believing." But it is not true: seeing is not believing. Any one can believe when he sees, but a Christian is to believe when he can**not see.** If not, what is the blessing of faith? or what **is** the gain of being a child of God? **We** dishonor our **Father if** we can believe in his goodness only when we can see goodness written out in large letters upon the things he gives. Goodness is always wrapped up even in the most painful experience our Father sends. **We** should never **lose** sight of the divine purpose **in** all trials—to make **our lives** more fruitful. Merely getting through troubles with quiet acquiescence is not all of true Christian endurance: we must seek to get through better men and women, with more of the mind and spirit of Christ, loving God and men more. We must see that the pruning makes us more fruitful—that the cutting away of earthly things or of human joys sends more of our life to spiritual things, and to the bearing of the fruits of righteousness and peace. A sorrow that does us no good only harms us.

XI.

FOR BETTER OR WORSE.

"O partner of my gladness, wife, what care, what grief, is there
For me you would not bravely face, with me you would not share?"

WILLIAM COX BENNETT.

ONE of the saddest things about life is the waste of its blessings. Hearts go hungry while close by, within easy reach, lies the bread which would satisfy their craving. The fainting fall in the struggle while close at hand are strong arms which could easily support them. Even in the closest relationships there is ofttimes a pitiful waste of joy and help. In many homes where hearts are really full of love the individuals fail to relate themselves to each other in such a way as to receive one from another what each yearns to give by sweet ministry. There are many marriages that fail to bring the wedded lives into that perfect union and communion whereby one life shares all its best with the other.

There are husbands who do not get the help from

their wives that their wives would love to give. They do not take them at all into their deepest, most real life. A man shares with his wife the pleasant things—the encouragements, the successes, the triumphs, the joys and prosperities. He talks over with her the light, easy things that he is doing. But the burdens, the discouragements, the adversities and the failures he does not tell her of, nor does he discuss with her the grave, serious questions that cause him perplexity and loss of rest.

It is not in an unkind or a selfish spirit that he withholds from her these trying and painful things; indeed, ofttimes it is the very tenderness of his regard for his wife that leads him to keep from her things that would cause her distress or anxiety of mind. He does not suppose that she could help him in the solving of the perplexing questions or in the bearing of the heavy burdens, and he thinks it would be unkindness in him to vex her with the questions or oppress her with the burdens. So he keeps these troublous things to himself, and ofttimes while he is in deep anxiety and bowing under heavy loads, wellnigh crushed beneath them, she is moving along in a path of sunshine, in quiet enjoyment, with no shadow of care, wholly unconscious of her husband's need of strong sympathy and help. Though the prompting of affection and of unselfishness in the husband, there is no doubt that in ordinary circumstances such a course is both wrong and unwise. It is robbing the wife of love's privilege of sharing the whole of her husband's life. It is treating her as if she were a child unable to understand the husband's affairs or to help him carry his load. It is taking from her the deep and exquisite joy which every true wife finds in suffering with her husband in whatever causes him pain or loss.

It is easy to find illustrations. Quite recently, in the case of a heavy business failure, the wife knew nothing whatever of the coming misfortune until it had actually fallen upon her home, sweeping all away. She then learned that for more than a year her husband had been struggling with his load, trying in every way to bring his affairs out of their complicated state and to escape the peril of bankruptcy. Meanwhile, his wife had been living in her sheltered home, wholly unaware of any stress or of any shadow impending. She had been spending money as freely as usual in her household management, making no effort to be economical, since she knew of no necessity for unwonted economy. Her neighbors and her neighbors' wives, knowing of her husband's business straits and of his almost certain failure in the near future, thought it strange that she still maintained her costly scale of household expenditure, making no effort whatever to be economical, and severely animadverted upon her want of sympathy with her husband in his financial distress. Had she known anything of the real condition of affairs, she would have instantly reduced her household outlay to the minimum, and possibly by doing this she might have saved him from failure. Besides, he would have had the inspiration of her loving, strengthening sympathy in all the struggle, and also the aid of her wifely counsel, enabling him to make a more heroic, if not a successful, struggle against adverse circumstances.

There is no doubt that in this case the husband's motive was unselfish and kindly. He shrank from giving anxiety and distress to his wife, and hoped to weather the storm without acquainting her with the fact that he was in a storm. His motive was generous, but his kindness was mistaken. He failed to honor her with that full confidence which every husband owes to the woman whom he has taken to his side as his wife. He inflicted positive injury and sore wrong upon her in allowing her to go on in her expensive style of living, ignorant of the stress of his circumstances, thus drawing upon herself the censure of her neighbors. This injustice to her was irreparable. Her name will never be altogether free from the reproach it gathered in those days of her husband's struggles when she seemed to be coldly indifferent to his distress. Yet for this reproach her husband alone was to blame.

When a man has taken a woman to be his wife, he has linked her life with **his** own in the closest of all earthly relations. Whatever concerns him also concerns her. **He** has no interests which are not hers as well as his. He should, therefore, make her the sharer of all his life. No remotest corner of it should be closed against her. She should know of his successes and triumphs and be permitted to rejoice with him in his gladness. **If** reverses come, she should know also of these, that she may sympathize with him, encourage and help **him** in his struggles and stand close beside him when the shadow rests upon him. They have linked their lives together "for better or worse," and they should share the pains and the trials as well as the pleasures and the comforts that come to either of them. A true wife is not a child; she is a woman, and should be treated as a woman.

There is resistless eloquence in the wife's appeal contained in the following lines:

> "Dear, it is twilight—the time of rest;
>   Ah! cease that weary pacing to and fro;
> Sit down beside me in this cushioned nest
>   Warm with the brightness of our ingleglow.
> Dear, thou art troubled. Let me share thy lot
>   Of shadow, as I shared thy sunshine hours:
> I am no child, though childhood, half forgot,
>   Lies close behind me, with its toys and flowers.
> I am a woman waked by happy love
>   To keep home's altar-fire alight;
> Thou hast elected me to stand above
>   All others in thine heart: I claim my right—
> Not wife alone, but mate and comrade true;
> I shared thy roses, let me share thy rue.
>
> "Bitter? I know it. God hath made it so,
>   But from his hand shall we take good alone,
> And evil never? Let the world's wealth go:
>   Life hath no loss which love cannot atone.
> Show me the new hard path which we must tread:
>   I shall not faint nor falter by the way;
> And, be there cloud or sunshine overhead,
>   I shall not fail thee to my dying day.
> But love me, love me! Let our hearts and lips
>   Cling closer in our sorrow than in joy;
> Let faith outshine our fortune in eclipse,
>   And love deem wealth a lost and broken toy.
> Joy made us glad, let sorrow find us true;
> God blessed our roses, he will bless our rue."

A man does deep injustice to the woman he has chosen to be his wife when he thinks that she is too frail and delicate to endure with him the storms **that blow upon** him, or that she is too inexperienced or too ignorant of life to discuss with him the problems **that** cause him grave **and** earnest thought. She may not have all his practical wisdom with regard to the world's affairs, and yet she may be able to offer many a suggestion **which** shall prove **of** more value to him than the counsel of shrewd men of the world. Woman's quick intuition often sees at **a** glance what **man's** slow logic is long in discovering. There is many a man whose success would have been greater far, or to whom failure would not have come, had he but sought or accepted his wife's counsel and help. Even if a wife can give no real practical aid, her husband will be made ten times stronger in his own heart by her strengthening sympathy and brave cheer while he is carrying his load or fighting his battle.

Whether, therefore, the day bring defeat or victory, failure or success, a man should confide all to his wife in the evening. If the day has been prosperous, she has a right to the gratification. If **it** has been adverse, she will want, as a **true,** heroic wife, to help **her husband** bear his burden **and to whisper** in his ear her word of loving cheer and encouragement.

Not only does a man fail to give his wife due honor when he shuts her out from participation in the struggles, conflicts, anxieties and disappointments of his life, but he also robs himself of that inspiration and help which every true and worthy wife earnestly longs to minister to the husband she loves. True marriage should unite husband and wife in their entire life, whether in joy or sorrow, in victory or defeat, in gain or loss. Then grief and loss, shared by wedded hearts, draws them closer together and renders their love richer, deeper, sweeter, stronger. As Lowell sings:

"I thought our love at full, but I did err;
    Joy's wreath dropped o'er my eyes: I could not see
    That sorrow in our happy world must be
Love's deepest spokesman and interpreter.
But, as a mother feels her child first stir
    Under her heart, so felt I instantly,
    Deep in my soul, another bond to thee
Thrill with that life I saw depart from her.
O mother of our angel-child! twice dear!
    Death knits as well as parts, and still, I wis,
Her tender radiance shall infold us here,
    Even as the light, borne up by inward bliss,
Threads the void glooms of space without a fear
    To print on farthest stars her pitying kiss."

There are possibilities of wedded happiness and of home blessedness which many husbands and wives fail to reach. It ought not to be so. Marriage is intended of God to be as nearly perfect as anything human can be in this world. It is a sad pity when the beautiful divine pattern is so marred in the weaving by clumsy hands, and when the wedded life so fails in the realizing of the ideal prophetically visioned in love's early dreams, that for love's blissful, joyous communion there is only cold toleration within the walls which ought to be sweet home.

This book may chance to find its way into the hands of some wedded pair whose hearts are sad through disappointment. They began their life together with large hopes and with almost heavenly dreams of happiness. But at every point they have failed. Their lives have not blended. Indeed, they have seemed to be held apart as if by some strange mutually-repellent force, forbidding their real union of soul. It appears to them now that they can never realize the sweet dreams which filled their hearts when they went to the marriage altar. Both are disheartened.

But surely there is no need for despair even in such a case as this. Longfellow tells in one of his poems of passing through the garden and seeing on the ground a fallen bird-nest, ruined and full of ruin. But, looking up into the tree above his head, he saw there the uncomplaining birds building among the branches a new nest for themselves instead of the one which had fallen to the ground. May not the poet's picture carry a fresh hope to husband and wife sitting in sad discouragement amid the shadows of a marriage that has failed? The nest has fallen out of the green branches and lies on the ground torn and desolated, but can they not yet build a new one more beautiful than the one that is in ruin, and in it make blessed joy and peace for themselves? God will help them if they will but come again to his feet to begin anew, and if they will but learn, at whatever cost of self-forgetfulness, love's holy secret.

XII.

"DOE YE NEXTE THYNGE."

"Do the work that's nearest
 Though it's dull at whiles."
                              CHARLES KINGSLEY.

"Comings and goings
 No turmoil need bring;
 His all thy future,
  'Doe ye nexte thynge.'"

DUTY never is a haphazard thing; it does not come to us in bundles from which we may choose what we like best. There are never a half dozen things either one of which we may fitly do at any particular time; there is some one definite and particular thing in the divine purpose for each moment. In writing music no composer strews the notes along the staff just as they happen to fall on this line or that space; he sets them in harmonious order and succession, so that they will make sweet music when played or sung. The builder does not fling the stones and the beams into the edifice without plan; every block and every piece of wood, stone or iron, and every brick, has its place and the building rises in graceful beauty.

The days are like the lines and spaces in the musical staff, and duties are the notes; each life is meant to be a perfect harmony, and in order to this each single duty has its own proper place. One thing done out of its time and place makes discord in the music of life, just as one note misplaced on the staff mars the harmony. Each life is a building, and the little acts are the materials used; the whole is congruous and beautiful only when every act is in its own true place. Everything is beautiful in its time, but out of time the loveliest acts lose much of their loveliness.

> "Far better in its place the lowliest bird
> Should sing aright to Him the lowliest song
> Than that a seraph strayed should take the word
> And sing his glory wrong."

The art of true living, therefore, consists largely in doing always the thing that belongs to the moment. But how to know what is the duty of each moment is a question which to many is full of perplexity. Yet it would be easy if our obedience were but more simple. We have but to take the duty that comes next to our hand—that which the moment brings. "Doe ye nexte thynge," says the quaint old **Saxon legend. Our** duty is never some **far-away** thing. We do not have to search **for it;** it is always close at hand and easily found. The trouble is that we complicate the question of duty for ourselves **by** our way of looking at life, **and** then get our feet entangled in the meshes which our own hands have woven.

Much of this confusion arises from taking too long views. We try to settle our duty in large sections. We think of years rather than of **moments,** of **life-work** rather than of individual acts. **It is** hard to plan a year's duty; it is easy to plan just for **one short day.** No shoulder can bear up the burden of a year's cares all gathered back **into** one load; the weakest shoulder can carry without weariness just what really belongs to one day. **In** trying to grasp the whole year's duty we are apt to overlook and to miss that of the present hour, just as one in gazing at a far-off mountain-top is likely not to see the little flower blooming at his feet, and even to tread it down as he stalks along.

There is another way in which many people complicate the question of duty. They try to reach decisions to-day on matters that really are not be**fore** them to-day, and that will not be before them for months—possibly for years. For example, a young man came to me the other day in very sore perplexity over a question of duty. He said he could not decide whether to go as a foreign missionary or to devote his life to work in some home-field. Yet he had but just closed his freshman year in college. It would require him three years to complete his college course, and then he would have to spend three years more in the theological seminary. Six years hence he would be ready for his work as a minister, and it was concerning his choice of field then that the young man was now in such perplexity. He said that often he passed hours on his knees in prayer, seeking for light, but that no light had come. He had even tried fasting, but without avail. The matter had so taken possession of his mind that he had scarcely been able to study during the last three months, and he had fallen behind his class. His health, too, he felt, was being endangered, as he often lay awake much of the night thinking upon the momentous question of his duty, as between home and foreign work.

It is very easy to see what was this young man's mistake: he was trying to settle now a question with which he had nothing whatever to do at the present time. If he is spared to complete his course of training, the question will emerge as a really practical **one five** or six years hence. It is folly for him now to try to compel a decision which he cannot make intelligently and without perplexity; from the fact that he cannot so make it, it is evi**dent** that the decision is no part of his present duty. He wonders that he can get no light upon the matter—that even in answer to agonizing prayer the perplexity does not grow less. But is there any ground to expect God to throw light on a man's path so far in advance of his steps? Is there any promise that prayer for guidance at a point so remote will be answered now? Why should it be? Will it not be time enough for the answer to come when the decision is really to be made?

Certainly it is right for the young man **to pray** concerning this matter, but his present request should be that God would direct his preparation so that he may be fitted for the work, whatever it may be, that in the divine purpose is waiting for him, and that at the proper time God would lead **him to** his allotted field. "Lord, prepare me for what thou art preparing for me," was the daily prayer of one young life. This is the fitting prayer for this Christian student; but to pray that he may know now where the Lord will send him to labor six years hence is certainly an unwarranted asking which is little short of presumption and of impertinent human intermeddling with divine things.

Another obvious element of mistake in this young man's case is that he is neglecting his present duty or failing to do it well while he is perplexing himself about what his duty will be several years hence. Thus he is hindering the divine purpose in his own preparation for the work his Master has planned for him. Life is not an hour too long; every moment of time allotted to us is necessary in realizing the divine plan for our lives. The preparatory years are enough, if they are faithfully used, in which to prepare for the years of life-work which come after. But every hour we waste leaves its own flaw in our preparation. Many people go halting and stumbling all through life, missing opportunities and continually failing where they ought to have succeeded, because they neglected their duty in the preparatory years.

The case of this student is typical of many. There are more persons who worry about matters that belong altogether to the future than there are who are anxious to do well the duty of the present moment. If we would simply do always the next thing, we would be relieved of all perplexity. This would also ensure our doing well whatever God gives us to do. Instead of looking far on for our duty, we would then find it always close before us. Instead of trying to make out what we ought to do next year or six years hence, we would ask only what we shall do the present hour. Instead of looking for our duty in large sections, we should then receive it in detail. The meaning of this rule of living is well illustrated in a little poem entitled

"'DOE YE NEXTE THYNGE.'

"From an old English parsonage
    Down by the sea
There came, in the twilight,
    A message to me;
Its quaint Saxon legend,
    Deeply engraven,
Hath, as it seems to me,
    Teaching from Heaven;
And through the hours
    The quiet words ring
Like a low inspiration:
    'Doe ye nexte thynge.'

"Many a questioning,
    Many a fear,
Many a doubt,
    Hath its quieting here.
Moment by moment,
    Let down from heaven,
Time, opportunity,
    Guidance, are given.

Fear not to-morrows,
  Child of the King;
Trust them with Jesus:
  'Doe ye nexte thynge.'

"Do it immediately,
  Do it with prayer,
Do it reliantly,
  Casting off care;
Do it with reverence,
  Tracing His hand
Who hath placed it before thee
  With earnest command.
Stayed on Omnipotence,
  Safe 'neath his wing,
Leave all resulting:
  'Doe ye nexte thynge.'"

By following this simple counsel the young student would devote himself with all his energy to the studies that belong to his present stage of progress. Possibly it may become quite plain to him early in his course that his work as a minister will be in a particular field; if so, this fact may shape in some sense his preparation. But if it still remains uncertain in what particular branch of ministerial service he is to labor, he should not give himself a moment's perplexity on the subject. Clearly, God holds this as yet unrevealed in his own hands. The student's duty is to make the best possible use of his present opportunities for study and self-discipline. At the right time he will have no difficulty in deciding where he is to work.

The law of divine guidance is, "Step by step." One who carries a lantern on a country-road at night sees only one step before him. If he takes that, he carries his lantern forward, and thus makes another step plain. At length he reaches his destination in safety, without once stepping into darkness. The whole way has been made light for him, though only a single step of it at a time. This illustrates the usual method of God's guidance. His word is represented as a lamp unto the feet. It is a lamp—not a blazing sun, nor even a lighthouse, but a plain, common lamp or lantern which one can carry about in the hand. It is a lamp "unto the feet," not throwing its beams afar, not illumining a hemisphere, but shining only on the one little bit of road on which the pilgrim's feet are walking.

If this is the way God guides, it ought never to be hard for us to find our duty. It never lies far away, inaccessible to us, but is always near—always "ye nexte thynge." It never lies out of our sight, in the darkness, for God never puts our duty where we cannot see it. The thing that we think may be our duty, but which is still lying in obscurity and uncertainty, is not our duty yet, whatever it may be a little farther on. The duty for the very moment is always clear, and that is as far as we need concern ourselves; for when we do the little that is clear, we will carry the light on, and it will shine on the next moment's step.

Miners carry their small lamps fastened to their caps. These lamps do not flood the whole great dark chamber of the mine where the men work, but they do light the one little spot where the miner has to strike his pick. Duty is a lamp, and as we move forward in quiet obedience we carry our own light with us, and thus never have to work in darkness, though it may be dense night close on all sides of us.

If not even one little step is plain to us, "ye nexte thynge" is to wait. Sometimes that is God's will for us. At least, it never is his will that we should take a step into the darkness. He never hurries us. We had better always wait than rush on as if we are not quite sure of the way. Often in our impatience we do rash things which we find after a little were not God's "nexte thynges" for us at all. That was Peter's mistake when he cut off a man's ear in the garden, and it led to sore trouble and humiliation a little **later.** There **are** many quick, impulsive people who are continually doing wrong next things, and who then find their *next* thing trying to undo the last. We must always wait for God, and never take a step which he has not made light for us.

> "To wait is naught
> When waiting means to serve."

Yet we must not be too slow; this danger is **as** great as that of being too quick. The people were never to go until the pillar moved; they were neither to run ahead nor **to** lag behind. Indolence is as bad as rashness. There are some people who are never on time. They never do things just when they ought to be done. They are continually in perplexity which of several things they ought to do first. The trouble is they are for ever putting **off** or neglecting or forgetting things, and consequently each morning **finds** them facing not only that day's duties, but the omitted duties of past days. There never really are two duties for the same moment; and if everything is done in its time, there never will be any perplexity in discover**ing** what is the right thing to do next.

It is a comfort to know that our duties are not

the accidents of any undirected flow of circumstances. We are plainly assured that if we acknowledge the Lord in all our ways he will direct our paths—that is, if we keep eye and heart ever turned toward God, we shall never be left to grope after the path, for it will be pointed out to us. We are authorized to pray that God would order our "steps;" what direction in duty could be more minute than that? Jesus said, "He that followeth me shall not walk in darkness." We must note well the Master's word: it is he that *followeth* him who shall not walk in darkness. We must not run on ahead of him, neither must we lag behind; in either case we shall find it darkness—just as deep darkness in advance of our Guide if we will not wait for him as it is behind him if we will not keep close up to him.

Prompt, unquestioning, undoubting following of Christ takes all the perplexity out of Christian life and gives unbroken peace. There is something for every moment, and duty is always "ye nexte thynge." It may sometimes be an interruption, setting aside a cherished plan of our own, breaking into a pleasant rest for which we had arranged or taking us away from a favorite occupation. It may be to meet a disappointment, to take up a cross, to

endure a sorrow or to pass through a trial. **It may be
to go up stairs and be sick for a time, letting go one's
hold on all active life, or it may be just the plainest,
commonest bit** of routine daily **work in the house,**
in the office, on the farm, at school. Most of **us**
find the greater number of our " next things " in
the tasks that are the same day after day, **yet even**
in the interstices amid these set tasks there come
a thousand little things of kindness, patience, gentleness, thoughtfulness, obligingness, like the sweet
flowers that **grow in** the crevices between the cold,
hard rocks, and **we** should always be ready for
these as **we** hurry along, **as** well as for the sterner
duties that our common calling brings to us.

There never is a moment without its duty; and
if we are living near to Christ and following him
closely, we shall never be left in ignorance **of** what
he wants us to do. If there is nothing—absolutely
nothing—for us to do at any time, then we may be
sure that the Master wants us to sit down a moment at his feet and rest. For he is not a hard
Master, and, besides, rest is as needful in its time
as work. We need to rest in order to work ; so **we**
must not worry when there come moments which
seem to have no task for **our** hands. The next
thing then is to sit down and rest a while.

XIII.
PEOPLE AS MEANS OF GRACE.

"May every soul that touches mine—
Be it the slightest contact—get therefrom some good,
Some little grace, one kindly thought,
One aspiration yet unfelt, one bit of courage
For the darkening sky, one gleam of faith
To brave the thickening ills of life,
One glimpse of brighter skies beyond the gathering mists
To make this life worth while
And heaven a surer heritage!"
Mrs. L. P. Sherman.

"Iron sharpeneth iron;
So a man sharpeneth the countenance of his friend."
Proverbs of Solomon.

THERE are pairs of pictures which show parties of Indian children and youth, first as they appeared when they came to Hampton or Carlisle, fresh from their barbarism, with the dress and all other marks of their savage state, then as they appeared after a time in the school, so transformed as to dress, expression of face and entire bearing as to be wellnigh, if not altogether, unrecognizable.

The change was wrought by the influences of Christian training and civilization, by contact with the lives of the men and women with whom they were associated as teachers and friends. It is not alone the instruction they have received that has so transformed these children of barbarism: it is the touch upon them of refined life and character. The blessing came to them not through books alone —not even through the Bible directly—but through other human lives which have themselves been leavened with the gentle and beautiful spirit of Jesus Christ.

We call prayer, Bible-reading, the Lord's Supper, and certain other specifically religious exercises, means of grace, but our list is quite too short. Anything that helps to interpret Christ to us and to bring us into closer relations with him; anything that becomes to us a disciplinary experience, drawing out and strengthening our life in any of its elements; anything that makes us better, holier, sweeter in spirit,—is to us a means of grace. Under this head, therefore, we may put work, which develops our powers; the struggle with trial and temptation, through which our natures are disciplined; the enduring of sorrow and pain, by which we are made more pure; and all experiences of life which result, or are designed to result, in the growth of our spiritual life.

Among other means of grace we must put our association with other people. In contact life with life we are impressed, wrought upon and influenced. Indeed, we receive the larger portion of our divine gifts through human hearts and lives. We sometimes overlook this and think of God as reaching down his mercies to us directly and immediately without the intervention of mediators. But closer thought shows us that ordinarily this is not the way our spiritual good things come to us. Ordinarily, God passes his gifts to us through others.

> "He hides himself within the love
>   Of those that we love best;
> The smiles and tones that make our homes
>   Are shrines by him possessed.
> He tents within the lowly heart
>   And shepherds every thought;
> We find him not by seeking long,
>   We lose him not unsought."

The Incarnation is the largest illustration of this truth. When God desired to reveal himself to men, he did not come down in flaming glory like Sinai's—the dazzling splendor would have blinded men's eyes—but manifested himself in a sweet and beautiful life. In human form Christ could come close to sinful men without awing or alarming them; and when they touched him, grace flowed from his lips and life to bless them.

What was true of this largest of all manifestations is true in lesser ways of all God's revealings. He does not open a window in heaven that we may look in and see his face. Even Christ does not come down and walk again upon our streets that we may see him as the disciples saw him: he makes himself known to us in and through the life of others. Even as in a dewdrop quivering on leaf or grass-blade on a summer's morning one can see the whole expanse of the blue sky, so in the lowliest life of a true believer there is a mirroring, though dim and imperfect, of the brightness of God's glory. Thus God reveals his love to a child through the love of the mother. Human parenthood is a little mirror in which the child sees reflected a vision of divine beauty. Thus the mother is the first means of grace to her child; she is the earliest interpreter to it of God's love and tenderness, of God's thoughtfulness and care, of God's holiness and authority.

The child is also a means of grace to the parent. Parents are set to train their children, to teach them about God and their duty and to build them up in character; but, while parents strive to do this sacred work for their children, the children in turn become teachers to their parents. A devout father and mother learn more of the love of God and of God's fatherhood as they bend over their first-born child or hold it in their arms than ever they had learned before from teachers and from books—even from the Bible. Their own feelings toward their child interpret God's feelings toward them; as their hearts warm toward their offspring and are thrilled with holy affection, they learn how the heart of the heavenly Father warms toward them and is thrilled with tenderness and yearning as he looks upon them.

In other ways, too, is a child a means of grace to its parents. Jesus set a little child in the midst of his disciples and bade them learn from it lessons of humility and simplicity. Every child that grows up in a true home is a constant teacher, and its opening life, like a rosebud in its unfolding, pours beauty and sweetness all about. Many a home has been transformed by the unconscious ministry of a little child.

Children are means of grace to parents, also, in the very care and anxiety which they cause. They are troubles as well as comforts. We have to work the harder to make provision for them; we have to deny ourselves when they come, **and begin to live for them.** They **cost** us many anxieties, **too**—sleepless nights, ofttimes, when they are **sick, days of** weariness when a thousand things have **to be done** for them. Then we have to plan for them and think of their education and training, and we have to teach them and look to the formation of their habits. In many cases, too, they cause sore anxiety **and** distress of heart by their waywardness and by our apprehension that they may not turn out well. In many homes the sorrow over the living is greater **far** than that for the dead who have passed to sweet rest.

> "Not for the dead, **O** Lord, we weep:
> Untroubled is their rest, and deep;
> For them why should we mourn or sigh?
> 'Neath quiet graves in peace they lie:
> **'Thou** givest thy beloved sleep.'
>
> "For tempted souls, for wand'ring sheep,
> For those whose path is rough and steep,—
> For these **we** lift our **voice on** high,
> Not for the dead."

Yet it is in these very experiences that our children become especially means of grace **to us.** We learn lessons of patience in our constant care for them. We are trained **to** unselfishness as, under the strong pressure of love, we are all the while denying ourselves and making personal sacrifices for them, doing all manner of serving for them. We are trained to gentler, softer moods as we witness their sufferings and as our hearts are pained by our anxieties on their behalf. Our distress as we watch them in their struggles and temptations and are grieved by their heedlessness and waywardness works its rich discipline in our own lives, teaching us compassion and faith as we cry to God for them. There really are no such growing-times in the lives of true Christian parents as when they are bringing up their children.

But not only are children thus means of grace to parents: the same is true of all lives in their influence one upon another. We learn many of our best lessons from our associations with our fellow-men. Every fragment of moral beauty in a regenerated life is a mirroring of a little fragment, at least, of the image of God on which our eyes may gaze. Every true Christian life is in an imperfect degree, and yet truly, a new incarnation: "Christ liveth in me." We cannot live with God, but we are permitted to live in very close and intimate relations with people who bear something of God's likeness. The good and the holy are therefore means of grace to us because they help to interpret to us the character and the will of God. In sympathetic fellowship with them we are made conversant with holiness in actual life, brought down out of the holy Book and incarnated before our eyes, and the effect is to produce like holiness in ourselves.

> "Meanwhile, with every son and saint of Thine
>   Along the glorious line,
> Sitting by turns beneath thy sacred feet,
>   We'll hold communion sweet—
> Know them by look and voice and thank them all
>   For helping us in thrall,
> For words of hope and bright examples given
> To show through moonless skies that there is light in heaven."

If living in direct spiritual communion with God is too high an experience for us, the next stage of privilege is living with others who are in constant intercourse with him. Converse with those who lie in Christ's bosom and know the secret of the Lord cannot but greatly enrich our own knowledge of divine things and elevate the tone of our own lives as we admire the purity, the truth, the goodness we see in them, and seek to attain these qualities for ourselves. One of the richest means of spiritual culture, therefore, is association with those whose lives are Christlike and the study of the biographies of the good and the holy who have gone from earth.

Then, even the faults and the infirmities of those with whom we come in contact may become to us means of grace. It is harder to live with disagreeable people than with those who are congenial, but the very hardness may become a discipline to us and help to develop in us the grace of patience. Association with quarrelsome, quick-tempered people may train us to self-control in speech, teaching us either to be silent under provocation or to give only the soft answer which turneth away wrath. Socrates had a wife—Xantippe—who, if history does not defame her, had a most violent temper. Socrates said he married her and endured her for self-discipline. No doubt his wife's temper was a means of cultivating self-control in him, and any one who may be similarly unfortunate in life's close associations should strive to use his misfortune as a means of gaining a full and complete conquest over himself. Thus even the evil in others may be made to yield its good and its blessings to us if only we rise to our opportunity.

Thus on all sides we find people means of grace to us. From the good and the saintly we get inspirations toward better things and are lifted up imperceptibly toward goodness and saintliness; from the gentle and the loving we receive softening influences which melt our hard, cold winter into the genial glow of summer; from the rude and the quarrelsome we get self-discipline in our continued effort, so far as in us lies, to live peaceably with them despite their disagreeableness and their disposition to contention. Friction polishes not only metals, but characters also. Iron sharpeneth iron; life sharpeneth life. People are means of grace to us.

We grow best, therefore, as Christians, in our true places in associated life. Solitariness is not good; in the broader as well as in the narrower sense it is not good for man to be alone. Every life needs solitude at times; we should all get into each of our busy days an hour of silence when human presences shall be shut away by the veil that shuts us in alone with God. We need such hours for quiet thought, for communion with Christ, for introspection, for spiritual feeding, for the drawing of blessing and holy influences down from heaven to replenish the waste produced by earth's toil, struggle and sorrow. There is a time for being alone, but we should not seek to live always nor usually in this way. Life in solitude grows selfish. The weeds of evil desire and unhealthy emotion flourish in solitariness.

We need to live among people that the best things in our lives may be drawn out in thought and care and service for others. It is by no means a good thing for us to live in such circumstances that we are not required to think of others, to make self-denials for others, and to live for others, not for ourselves. The greater and more constant the pressure toward unselfishness, toward looking out and not in, and lending a hand, the better for the true growth and development of our lives. We never become unselfish save under conditions that compel us to live unselfishly. If we live—as we may live—with heart and life open to every good influence, we get some blessing, some inspiration, some warning, some touch of beauty, some new drawing out of latent life, some fresh uplift, from every person we meet, even most casually. There is no life with which we come in contact which may not bring us some message from God or by its very faults and infirmities help to discipline us into stronger, calmer, deeper, truer life, and thus become to us a means of grace.

XIV.

SHALL WE WORRY?

> "The little worries which we meet each day
> May lie as stumbling-blocks across our way,
> Or we may make them stepping-stones to be
> Of grace, O Lord, to thee."
>
> A. E. HAMILTON.

WHEN you are inclined to worry—don't do it. That is the first thing. No matter how much reason there seems to be for worrying, still, there is your rule. Do not break it: don't worry. Matters may be greatly tangled, so tangled that you cannot see how they ever can be straightened out; still, don't worry. **Troubles may be very real** and very sore, and there **may not** seem **a rift** in the clouds; nevertheless, don't worry.

You say the rule is too high for human observance—that mortals cannot reach it; or you say there must be some exceptions to it—that there are peculiar circumstances in which one cannot but worry. But wait a moment. What did the Master teach? "I say unto you, be not anxious for your life. . . . Be not anxious for the morrow." He left no exceptions. What did St. Paul teach? "In nothing be anxious." He said not a word about exceptions to the rule, but left it unqualified and absolute. A good bit of homely, practical, common-sense wisdom says that there are two classes of things we should not worry about—things we can help, and things we cannot help. Evils we can help we ought to help. If the roof leaks, we ought to mend it; if the fire is burning low and the room growing cold, we ought to put on more fuel; if the fence is tumbling down, so as to let our neighbor's cattle into our wheat-field, we had better repair the fence than sit down and worry over the troublesomeness of people's cows; if we have dyspepsia and it makes us feel badly, we had better look to our diet and our exercise. That is, we are very silly if we worry about things we can help. Help them. That is the heavenly wisdom for that sort of ills or cares: that is the way to cast that kind of burden on the Lord.

But there are things we cannot help. "Which of you by being anxious can add one cubit unto his stature?" What folly, then, for a short man to worry because he is not tall, or for a woman to worry about the color of her hair, or for any one to worry because of any physical peculiarities he may have? These are types of a large number of things in people's lives which no human power can change. Why worry about these? Will worrying do any good? So we come to the same result by applying this common-sense rule. Things we can make better we should make better, and not fret about them; and things we cannot help or change we should accept as God's will for us, and make no complaint about them. This very simple principle, faithfully applied, would eliminate all worrying from our lives.

As children of our heavenly Father we may go a step farther. If this world were governed by chance, no amount either of philosophy or of common sense could keep us from worrying; but we know that our Father is taking care of us. No little child in truest and most sheltered home was ever carried so closely or so safely in the love and thought and care of earthly parents as is the least of God's little ones in the heavenly Father's heart. The things we cannot help or change are in his hand, and belong to the "all things" which, we are assured, "work together for good to them that love God." In the midst of all the great rush of events and circumstances in which we can see no order and no design we well know that each believer in Christ is as safe as any little child in the arms of the most loving mother. It is not a mere blind faith that we try to nourish in our hearts as we seek to school ourselves to quietness and confidence amid all life's trials and disappointments: it is a faith that rests upon the character and the infinite goodness of God —the faith of a little child in a Father whose name is "Love" and whose power extends to every part of his universe. So here we find solid rock upon which to stand, and good reason for our lesson that we should never worry. Our Father is taking care of us. This argument is well expressed in the following lines:

> "If I could only surely know
> That all the things that tire me so
>   Were noticed by my Lord—
> The pang that cuts me like a knife,
> The lesser pains of daily strife—
>   What peace it would afford!

> "I wonder if he really shares
> In all these little human cares,
>   This mighty King of kings?
> If He who guides through boundless space
> Each blazing planet in its place
> Can have the condescending grace
>   To mind these petty things?

"It seems to me, if sure of this,
　　Blent with **each ill** would come such bliss
　　　That I might covet pain,
　　And deem whatever brought to me
　　The loving thought of Deity
　　And sense of Christ's sweet sympathy,
　　　Not loss, but richest gain.

"Dear Lord, my heart shall no more doubt
　　That thou dost compass me about
　　　With sympathy divine;
　　The Love for me once crucified
　　Is not the love to leave my side,
　　But waiteth ever to divide
　　　Each smallest care of mine."

But if **we** are never to worry, what shall we do with the **things** that incline us to anxiety? There are many such things in the life even of the most warmly sheltered. There are disappointments that leave the hands empty after days and years of **hope** and toil; there are resistless thwartings of fondly-cherished plans and purposes; there are bereavements that seem to sweep away every earthly joy; **there** are perplexities through which no **human** wisdom can lead the feet; there are experiences in **every life** whose natural effect is **to perturb the** spirit **and** produce deep and painful anxiety. If we **are** never to worry, what **are** we to do with **these** things that naturally tend to cause us worry?

The answer is easy: we are to put all these disturbing and distracting things into the hands of God. Of course, if we carry them ourselves, we cannot help worrying over them. But we are not to carry them; we cannot if we would. Up to the measure of our wisdom and our ability we are to forecast our lives and shape our circumstances. What people sometimes call trust is only indolence; we must meet life heroically. But when we have done our whole simple duty, there both our duty and our responsibility end. We cannot hold back the wave that the sea flings upon the beach; we cannot control the winds and the clouds and the other forces of nature; we cannot keep away the frosts that threaten to destroy our summer fruits; we cannot shut out of our doors the sickness that brings pain and suffering or the sorrow that leaves its poignant anguish; we cannot prevent the misfortune that comes through others or through public calamity. In the presence of all this class of ills we are utterly powerless; they are irremediable by any wisdom or strength of ours. Why, then, should we endeavor to carry them, only to vex ourselves in vain with them?

Besides, there is no reason why we should even try to carry them. It would be a very foolish little child in a home of plenty and **of love that** should worry about its food and raiment or about its father's business-affairs, and be all the while in a state **of** anxiety and distress concerning its own safety and comfort. The child has nothing whatever to do with these matters; its father **and** its mother are attending to them.

Or imagine a great ship on the ocean and **the** child of the ship's captain on board. The child goes about the vessel anxious concerning every movement **and** worried **lest** something may **go** wrong—lest the engines may fail, or the sails give **out, or** the sailors not do their duty, or the provisions become exhausted, or the machinery break down. What has the captain's child to do with any of these things? The child's father is looking after them.

We are God's children, living in our Father's world, and we have nothing more to do with the world's affairs than the shipmaster's little child has to do with the management and care of the great vessel in mid-ocean. We have only to stay in our place and attend to our own little personal duties, giving ourselves no shadow of anxiety about **anything** else. That is what we **are** to do instead of worrying when we meet things that would naturally perplex us. We are just to lay them in God's hands—where they belong—that he may look after them while we abide in quiet peace and go on with our little daily duties.

We have high scriptural authority for this. This is what St. Paul teaches in his immortal prison-letter, when he says, " Be careful [or anxious] for nothing ; but in everything by prayer and supplication, with thanksgiving, let your requests be made known unto God. And the peace of God, which passeth all understanding, shall keep your hearts and your minds through Christ Jesus." The points here shine out very clearly. We are to be anxious in nothing, in no possible circumstances—are never to worry. Instead of being anxious, we are to take everything to God in prayer. The result will be peace : " The peace of God shall keep your hearts and your minds through Christ Jesus." St. Peter's counsel is similar, though more condensed. In the Revised Version its meaning comes out more clearly : " Casting all your anxiety upon him, because he careth for you." God is taking care of you, not overlooking the smallest thing, and you have but to cast all your anxiety upon him and then be at peace. It is trying to carry our own cares that produces worry ; our duty is to cast them all upon Christ, giving ourselves thought only about our duty. **This is the secret of peace.**

There is a practical suggestion which may be helpful in learning this lesson. The heart in its pressure of care or pain cannot well remain silent; it must speak or break. Its natural impulse **is to** give utterance to its emotion in cries of pain or in fretful complainings and discontented murmurings. It will be a great relief to the overburdened **spirit if in** time of pain or trial the pent-up feelings can be given some other vent than **in** expressions **of** worry or anxiety. It is most suggestive, therefore, that in St. Paul's words, already quoted, when he says we should take our anxieties to God in prayer, he adds "with thanksgiving." The songs of thanksgiving carry off the heart's suppressed pain and give it relief.

In *Marble Faun*, Hawthorne makes Miriam, the broken-hearted singer, in the midnight song that went up from the Roman Coliseum, put into the melody the pent-up shriek to which her anguish had almost given vent a moment before: "That volume of melodious voice was one of the tokens of a great trouble. The thunderous anthem gave her an opportunity to relieve her heart by a great cry." It is better always to put pain or grief into melody than into wails. It is better for the heart itself; it is a sweeter relief. There are no wings like the wings of song and praise to bear away life's burdens. Then it is better for the world to start a song trembling in its air than to set loose a shriek or a cry of anguish to fly abroad.

We remember that our Lord, when he was nailed on the cross, where his sufferings must have been excruciating, instead of a cry of anguish turned the woe of his heart into a prayer of intercession for his murderers. St. Paul, too, in his prison, his back torn with the scourge and his feet fast in the stocks, uttered no word of complaint and no cry of pain, but gave vent to his great suffering in midnight hymns of praise which rang through all the prison.

These illustrations suggest a wonderful secret of heart-peace in the time of distress, from whatever cause. We must find some outflow for our pent-up emotions; silence is unendurable. We may not complain nor give utterance to feelings of anxiety, but we may turn the bursting tides into the channels of praise and prayer.

Then, we may also find relief in loving service for others. Indeed, there is no more wonderful secret of joyful endurance of trial than this. If the heart can put its pain or its fear into helping and comforting those who are in need and in trouble, it soon forgets its own care. If the whole inner story of lives were known, it would be found that many of those who have done the most to comfort the world's sorrow and bind up its wounds and help it in its need have been men and women whose own hearts found outlet for their pain, care or sorrow in ministries to others in Christ's name. Thus they found blessing for themselves in the peace that ruled in their lives, and they became blessings to the world by giving it songs instead of tears, and helpful service instead of the burden of discontent and complaining.

If a bird has to be in a cage, it is better to be a canary to fill its place of imprisonment with happy song than to be a starling to sit dumb within the wire walls in inconsolable distress. If we must have cares and trials, it is better that we should be rejoicing Christians, brightening the very darkness of our environment with the bright light of Christian faith, than that we should succumb to our troubles and get nothing but worry out of our life, and give nothing to the world but murmurings and the memory of our miserable discontent.

XV.

A WORD ABOUT TEMPER.

"Help us, O Lord! with patient love to bear
　　Each other's faults, to suffer with true meekness;
Help us each other's joys and griefs to share,
　　But let us turn to thee alone in weakness."

MORE than half of us are bad-tempered—at least so an English philosopher tells us. He claims that this is no mere general statement and no bit of guesswork; he gives us the figures for it. He arranged to have about two thousand people put unconsciously under espionage as to their ordinary temper, and then had careful reports made of the results. The footing up of the returns has been announced, and is decidedly unflattering to the two thousand tempers that were thus put to the test. More than half of these people—to be entirely accurate, fifty-two *per centum* of them—are set down as bad-tempered in various degrees. The dictionary has been wellnigh exhausted of adjectives of this order in giving the different shades of badness.

Acrimonious, aggressive, arbitrary, bickering, capricious, captious, choleric, contentious, crotchety, **despotic**, domineering, easily offended, gloomy, grumpy, hasty, huffy, irritable, morose, obstinate, **peevish**, sulky, **surly**, vindictive,—these **are some of the** qualifying words. There are employed, in all, **forty**-six terms, none of which describes a sweet **temper.**

We do not like to believe that the case is quite so serious—that a little more than every second one of us is unamiable in some offensive degree. It is easier to confess **our** neighbor's faults and infirmities than our own; so, therefore, quietly taking refuge for ourselves among the forty-eight *per centum* of good-tempered people, **we** shall probably be willing **to** admit that a great many of the people we know have at times rather ungentle tempers. They **are** easily provoked; they fly into a passion on very slight occasion; they are haughty, domineering, peevish, fretful or vindictive.

What is even worse, most of them appear to make no effort to grow out of their infirmities of disposition. The sour fruit does not come to mellow ripeness in the passing years; the roughness is not polished off the diamond to reveal its lustrous hidden beauty. The same petulance, pride, vanity, selfishness and other disagreeable qualities are found in the life year after year. Where there is a struggle to overcome one's faults and grow out of them, and where the progress toward better and more beautiful spiritual character is perceptible, though ever so slow, we should have patience; but where one appears unconscious of one's blemishes and manifests no desire to conquer one's faults there is little ground for encouragement.

> "Manlike is it to fall into sin:
> Fiendlike is it to dwell therein;
> Christlike is it for sin to grieve;
> Godlike is it all sin to leave."

Bad temper is such a disfigurement of character, and, besides, works such harm to one's self and to one's neighbors, that no one should spare any pains or cost to have it cured. The ideal Christian life is one of unbroken kindliness. It is dominated by love—the love whose portrait is drawn for us in the immortal thirteenth of First Corinthians. It suffereth long and is kind. It envieth not. It vaunteth not itself, is not puffed up, doth not behave itself unseemly, seeketh not its own, is not provoked, taketh not account of evil; beareth all things, believeth all things, hopeth all things, endureth all things. That is the picture; then we have but to turn to the gospel pages to find the story of a Life in which all this was realized. **Jesus never lost his temper.** **He** lived among people who tried him at every point—some by their dullness, others **by** their bitter enmity and persecution—but **he never** failed in sweetness of disposition, in long-suffering patience, in self-denying love. Like **the flowers** which give out their perfume only when crushed, like the odoriferous wood which bathes with fragrance the axe which hews it, the life **of** Christ yielded only the tenderer, sweeter love to the rough impact of men's rudeness and wrong. That is the pattern on which we should strive **to** fashion our life and our **character.** **Every** outbreak of violent temper, every shade of ugliness in disposition, mars the radiant loveliness of the picture we are seeking to have fashioned in our souls. Whatever is **not** loving is unlovely.

There is another phase: bad-tempered people are continually hurting others, ofttimes their best and truest friends. Some people are sulky, and one per**son's** sulkiness casts a chilling shadow over a whole household; others are so sensitive, ever watching for slights and offended by the merest trifles, that even their nearest friends have no freedom of intercourse with them; others are despotic, and will brook no kindly suggestion nor listen to any expression of opinion; others are so quarrelsome that even the meekest and gentlest person cannot live peaceably with them. Whatever may be the special characteristic of the bad temper, it makes only pain and humiliation for the person's friends.

A bad temper usually implies a sharp tongue. Sometimes, indeed, it makes one morose and glum. A brother and a sister living together are said often to have passed months without speaking to each other, though eating at the same table and sleeping under the same roof. A man recently died who for twelve years, it was said, had never spoken to his wife, though they continued to dwell together, and three times daily sat down together at the same table. Bad temper sometimes runs to proud silence. Such silence is not golden. Generally, however, a bad-tempered person has an unbridled tongue and speaks out his hateful feelings; and there is no limit to the pain and the harm which angry and ugly words can produce in gentle hearts.

> "These clumsy feet, still in the mire,
>   Go crushing blossoms without end;
> These hard, well-meaning hands we thrust
>   Among the heart-strings of a friend.
>
> "The ill-timed truth we might have kept—
>   Who knows how sharp it pierced and stung?

> The word we had not sense to say—
> Who knows how grandly it had rung ?"

It would be easy to extend this portrayal of the evils of bad temper, but it will be more profitable to inquire how a bad-tempered person may become good-tempered. There is no doubt that this happy change is possible in any case. There is no temper so obdurately bad that it cannot be trained into sweetness. The grace of God can take the most unlovely life and transform it into the image of Christ. As in all moral **changes,** however, grace does not work independently **of** human volition and exertion: **God** always works helpfully **with** those who strive to reach Christlikeness. **We must** resist the devil, or he will not flee from **us. We** must struggle to obtain the victory over our own evil habits and dispositions, although it is only through Christ that we can be conquerors; he will not make us conquerors unless we enter the battle. We have a share, and a large and necessary share, **in the culture of our own** character. **The** bad-**tempered** man will never become good-tempered until he deliberately sets for himself the task and enters resolutely and persistently upon its **accom-**plishment. The transformation will never come of itself even in a Christian. People do not grow out of ugly temper into sweet refinement as a peach ripens from sourness into lusciousness.

Then the thing to be accomplished is not the destroying of the temper: temper is a good quality in its place. The task is not destruction, but control. A man is very weak who has a strong temper without the power of self-control; likewise is he weak who has a weak temper. The truly strong man is he who is strong in the element of temper—that is, has strong passions and feelings capable of great anger, and then has perfect self-control. When Moses failed and broke down in temper, self-control, he was not the man to lead the people into the Promised Land; therefore God at once prepared to relieve him. The task to be set, therefore, in self-discipline is the gaining of complete mastery over every feeling and emotion, so as to be able to restrain every impulse to speak or to act unadvisedly.

Then there is need of a higher standard of character in this regard than many people seem to set for themselves. We never rise higher than our ideals; the perfect beauty of Christ should ever be visioned in our hearts as that which we would attain for ourselves. The honor of our Master's name should impel us to strive ever toward Christlikeness in spirit and in disposition. We represent Christ in this world; people cannot see him, and they must look at us to see a little of what he is like. Whatever great work we may do for Christ, if we fail to live out his life of patience and forbearance, we fail in an essential part of our duty as Christians. "The servant of the Lord must be . . . gentle."

Nor can we be greatly useful in our personal life while our daily conduct is stained by frequent outbursts of anger and other exhibitions of temper. In the old fable the spider goes about doing mischief wherever it creeps, while the bee by its wax and its honey makes "sweetness and light" wherever it flies. We had better be bees than be spiders, living to turn darkness into light and to put a little more sweetness into the life of all who know us. But only as our own lives shine in the brightness of holy affectionateness and our hearts and lips distill the sweetness of patience and gentleness can we fulfill our mission in this world as Christ's true messengers to men.

In striving to overcome our impatience with others it will help us to remember that we and they have the common heritage of a sinful nature. The thing in them which irritates us is, no doubt, balanced by something in us which looks just as unlovely in their eyes and just as sorely tries their forbearance toward us. Whittier wisely says:

> "Search thine own heart. What paineth thee
> In others, in thyself may be.
> All dust is frail, all flesh is weak:
> Be thou the true man thou dost seek."

Very likely, if we think our neighbors hard to live peaceably with, they think about the same of us; and who shall tell in whom lies the greater degree of fault? Certain it is that a really good-tempered person can rarely ever be drawn into a quarrel with any one. He is resolutely determined that he will not be a partner in any unseemly strife; he would rather suffer wrongfully than offer any retaliation; he has learned to bear and to forbear. Then by his gentle tact he is able to conciliate any who are angry.

A fable relates that in the depth of a forest there lived two foxes. One of them said to the other one day in the politest of fox-language, "Let's quarrel."—"Very well," said the other; "but how shall we set about it?" They tried all sorts of ways, but in vain, for both would give way. At last one brought two stones. "There!" said he. "Now you say they are yours and I'll say they are mine, and we will quarrel and fight and scratch.

Now I'll begin. Those stones are mine."—"All right!" answered the other fox; "you are welcome to them."—"But we shall never quarrel at this rate," replied the first.—"No, indeed, you old simpleton! Don't you know it takes two to make a quarrel?" So the foxes gave up trying to quarrel, and never played again at this silly game.

The fable has its lesson for other creatures besides foxes. As far as in us lies, St. Paul tells us, we should live peaceably with all men. A wise man says, "Every man takes care that his neighbors shall not cheat him, but a day comes when he begins to care that he does not cheat his neighbors. Then all goes well. He has changed his market-cart into a chariot of the sun." So long as a man sees only the quarrelsome temper of his neighbor he is not far toward saintliness; but when he has learned to watch and to try to control his own temper and to weep over his own infirmities, he is on the way to God, and will soon be conqueror over his own weakness.

There is one place where our impatience, irritability and ill-temper cannot but shame us. Says the Quaker poet, again:

"My heart was heavy, for its trust had been
 Abused, its kindness answered with foul wrong;

> So, turning gloomily from my fellow-men,
>   One summer Sabbath day I strolled along among
> The green mounds of the village burial-place,
>   Where, pondering how all human love and hate
>   Find one sad level, and how, soon or late,
> Wronged and wrong-doer, each with meekened face
>   And cold hands folded over a still heart,
> Pass the green threshold of our common grave,
>   Whither all footsteps tend, whence none depart,—
> Awed for myself and pitying my race,
> Our common sorrow like a mighty wave
> Swept all my pride away, and trembling I forgave."

Life is too short to spend even one day of it in bickering and strife; love is too sacred to be for ever lacerated and torn by the ugly briers of sharp temper. Surely we ought to learn to be patient with others, since God has to show every day such infinite patience toward us. Is not the very essence of true love the spirit that is not easily provoked, that beareth all things? Can we not, then, train our life to sweeter gentleness? Can we not learn to be touched even a little roughly without resenting it? Can we not bear little injuries and apparent injustices without flying into an unseemly rage? Can we not have in us something of the mind of Christ which will enable us, like him, to endure all wrong and injury and give back no word or look of bitterness? The way over which we and our friend walk together is too short to be spent in wrangling.

> "**They are** such dear familiar feet that go
> Along the path with ours—feet fast or slow,
> And trying **to keep** pace. If they mistake,
> Or tread upon some flower that we would take
> Upon our breast, or bruise some reed,
> Or crush poor hope until it bleed,
> We may be mute,
> Not turning quickly to impute
> Grave fault; for they and we
> Have such **a little** way to go—can be
> Together such a little while along the way—
> We will be patient while **we may.**
>
> "**So** many little faults we find!
> **We see** them, **for** not blind
> **Is love.** We see them; but if you and I
> Perhaps remember them some by and by,
> They will not be
> Faults then—grave faults—to you and me,
> But just odd ways, mistakes, or even less—
> Remembrances to bless.
> Days change so many things—yes, hours;
> We **see** so differently **in** sun **and** showers.
> Mistaken words to-night
> **May be so cherished by to-morrow's light.**
> We may be patient, for we know
> There's such a little way to go."

XVI.

FORWARD, AND NOT BACK.

> "Arouse thee, soul!
> Oh, there is much to do
> For thee if thou wouldst work for humankind!
> The misty future through
> A greatness looms: 'tis mind—awakened mind!
> Arouse thee, soul!"
>
> Robert Nicoll.

IT is a good thing always to face forward. Even nature shows that men's eyes were designed to look always "to the fore," for no man has eyes in the back of his head, as all men certainly would have if it had been intended that they should spend much time in looking backward. We like to have Bible authority for our rules in life, and there is a very plain word of Scripture which says,

> "Let thine eyes look right on,
> And let thine eyelids look straight before thee."

There is also a striking scriptural illustration in the greatest of the apostles, who crystalized the central principle of his active life in the remarkable words, "This one thing I do, forgetting those things which are behind, and reaching forth unto those things which are before, I press toward the mark." The picture is of a man running in the race-course. He sees only one thing—the goal yonder. He does not trouble himself to look back to see how far he has come or how far the other runners are behind him; he does not even look to the right hand or to the left to catch glimpses of his friends who are watching him and cheering him: his eyes look right on to the goal, while he bends every energy to the race.

That is the picture St. Paul drew of himself as a man, as a Christian; he forgot his past, and lived only for his future. We must remember, too, that he was an old man when he wrote these words; looking at him, we would say there was but little before him now to live for—but little margin of life left to him. The young look forward naturally, because everything is before them: the long, bright future years seem to stretch out for them almost illimitably; they live altogether in hope, and as yet have no memories to draw their eyes and their hearts backward and to chain their lives to the past. But old people, who have spent most of their allotted years and have but a small and fast-crumbling edge of life remaining, are much prone to live almost entirely in the past. The richest treasures of their hearts are there, left behind and passed by, and so their eyes and their thoughts are drawn backward rather than forward.

Here, however, was one old man who cared nothing for what was past, and who lived altogether in hope, pressing on with quenchless enthusiasm into the future. What was gone was nothing to him in comparison with what was yet to come. The best things in his life were still to be won; his noblest achievements were yet to be wrought; his soul was still full of visions unrealized which would yet be realized. His eye pierced death's veil, for to him life meant immortality, and earth's horizon was not its boundary. The last glimpse we have of this old man he is about going forth from his Roman dungeon to martyrdom, but he is still reaching forth and pressing on into the Before. His keen eye is fixed on a glory which other men could not see as with exultation he cried, "The time of my departure is at hand. . . . Henceforth there is laid up for me a crown."

There is something very sublime in such a life, and it ought to have its inspirations for us. We ought to train ourselves to live by the same rule.

There is a tremendous waste in human energy **and in all life's** powers resulting **from** the habit of ever turning to look backward. While we stand thus, with arms folded, peering back into the mists and the shadows of the dead past, the great, resistless, never-resting tides of life are sweeping on, and we are simply left behind. And few things are sadder than this—men with their powers yet at their best left behind in the race and left alone because they **stop** and stand and look backward instead of keeping their eyes to the front and bravely pressing on to the things before.

It is every way better to look forward than to look back. The life follows the eye; we live as we look. But what is there ever behind us to live for? There is no work to do; no tasks wait there for accomplishment; no opportunities for helpfulness or usefulness lie in the past. Opportunities, when once they have passed by, never linger that tardy laggards may yet come up and seize them; passed once, they are gone for ever. Rose Terry Cooke writes:

> "Never comes the chance that passed:
> That one moment was its last.
> Though thy life upon it hung,
> Though thy death beneath it swung,

> If thy future all the way
> Now in darkness goes astray,
> When the instant born of fate
> Passes through the golden gate,
> When the hour, but not the man,
> Comes and goes from Nature's plan,—
> Nevermore its countenance
> Beams upon thy slow advance;
> Nevermore that time shall be
> Burden-bearer unto thee.
> Weep and search o'er land and main,
> Lost chance never comes again."

We cannot impress ourselves in any way upon the past; the records which are written all over the pages of yesterday were made when yesterday was the living present. We cannot make any change on the past; we can undo nothing there, correct nothing, erase nothing. We may get a measure of inspiration from other men's past as we study their biographies and their achievements and grasp the secrets of their power.

> "Lives of great men all remind us
> We can make our lives sublime,
> And, departing, leave behind us
> Footprints on the sands of time."

Then, we may get something, too, from our own past in the lessons of experience which we have learned. He certainly lives very heedlessly whose days yield no wisdom; yesterday's mistakes **and failures** should make the way plainer and straighter to-day. Past sorrows, too, should enrich our lives. **All** one's past is in the life of each new day—all its spirit, **all** its lessons, all its accumulated wisdom, all **its** power—lives in each present moment. **Yet this benefit** that comes from the things that are **behind** avails only when it becomes impulse and energy **to send us** forward the more resistlessly and wisdom **to guide us the more** safely.

> "**Let the** dead past bury its dead:
> **Act, act** in the living present."

Therefore **we** should never waste a moment in looking back at our past attainments. Yet there are people who, especially in their later years, do little else. They are accomplished egotists, yet they never have anything but very old heroisms and achievements **to talk** about. They are garrulous enough concerning the great things they have done, **but it** was always **a** long time ago that they did them. **All** the grand and noble things in their **life are** little **more** than traditions. Their religious experiences, also, are of old date, and they seem never **to** have any new ones. Their testimonies and their prayers in the conference-meeting are quite like the tunes of street-organs—the same always every time you hear them; they never get a new tune, not even a new and revised edition of the old one. With mechanical invariableness and endless repetition they relate the same experiences year after year. They can tell a great deal about what they felt and what they did a long time ago, but not a word about what they felt and what they did yesterday.

The utter inadequacy and the unworthiness of such living are apparent at a glance. No past glory avails for this living present. The radiance of last night will not make the stars brilliant to-night; the beauty of last summer's flowers will not do for the flowers of this summer; the industry of early manhood will not achieve results in mid-life or in old age; the heroism of yesterday will win no laurels for the brow to-day. What matters it that one did great things some time in the past? The question is, What is he doing now? Suppose a man had ecstatic experiences ten or twenty years ago; ought he not to have had still more ecstatic experiences every year since? Suppose a man did a noble thing twenty-five years ago; why should he still sound the praises of that one lone deed after so long a lapse of time? Ought he not to have done just as noble things all along his life as he did that particular day a quarter-century since? The ideal life is one that does its best every day, **and** sees ever in to-morrow an opportunity for something better than to-day. **It** is sad when any one has to look back for his best achievements and his highest attainments. However lofty the plane reached, the face should still be turned forward and **the heart** should still be reaching onward for its best.

The true **life** has its image in the tree which **drops its** ripe fruits in the autumn and forgets them, leaving them to be food for the hungry, while it straightway begins to prepare for another year's fruits. **What an** abnormal thing it would be for an apple tree to bear an abundant crop and then never again produce anything but, each year, a few scattered apples hanging lonesome on the widespreading branches, while the tree continued to glory year after year in its superb yield of long ago! Is such a life any more fitting for an immortal man than for a soulless fruit tree? Immortal**ity** should never content itself with any past. Not back, but forward, always should our eyes be bent. The years should be ladder-steps upward, each lifting us higher. Even death should not intercept **the** onward look, for surely the best things are never this side, but always on beyond death's mists. Death is not a wall cutting off the path and ending all progress: it is a gate—an open gate—through which the life sweeps on through eternity. Progress, therefore, is endless, and the goal is ever unreached.

Even the mistakes and the sins of the past should not draw our eyes back. Sins should instantly be confessed, repented of and forsaken, and that should be the end. To brood over them does no good; we can never undo them, and no tears can obliterate the fact of their commission. The way to show true sorrow for wrong-doing is not to sit in sackcloth and ashes weeping over the ruin wrought, but to pour all the energy of our regret into new obedience and better service. The past we cannot change, but the future we can yet make beautiful if we will. It would be sad if in weeping over the sins of yesterday we should lose to-day also. Not an instant, therefore, should be wasted in unavailing regret when we have failed; the only thing to do with mistakes is not to repeat them, while, at the same time, we set about striving to get some gain or blessing from them.

Defeats in life should never detain us long, since only faith and courage are needed to change them into real victories. **For,** after all, it is **character** we are building in this world; and if we use every experience to promote our growth, to make us **better,** if we emerge **from** it stronger, braver, **truer, nobler,** we have lost nothing, **but** have been the gainer. In reverses and misfortunes, then, **we have but** to keep our eyes fixed on Christ, caring only that no harm comes to our soul from the loss **or the trial,** and thus we shall be victorious. **If** we stop **and look back with** despairing heart at the wreck of **our hopes and** plans, our defeat will **be** real and humiliating; like Lot's wife, we shall be buried beneath the encrusting salt. **But if we** resolutely turn away from the failure or the **ruin** and press on **to** brighter things—things that cannot perish—we shall get victory and win **blessedness** and eternal **gain.** "Look forward, and not back." Live to make to-morrow beautiful, not to stain yesterday with tears **of** regret and grief.

> " Out of **the** twilight of the **past**
> We move to a diviner light:
> **For** nothing that is wrong can last;
> **Nothing's immortal but** the right."

XVII.
THE DUTY OF FORGETTING SORROW.

"Thou knowest that through our tears
  Of hasty, selfish weeping
Comes surer sin, and for our petty fears
  Of loss thou hast in keeping
A greater gain than all of which we dreamed;
  Thou knowest that in grasping
The bright possessions which so precious seemed
  We lose them; but if, clasping
Thy faithful hand, we tread with steadfast feet
  The path of Thy appointing,
There waits for us a treasury of sweet
  Delight, royal anointing
With oil of gladness and of strength."

HELEN HUNT JACKSON.

SORROW makes deep scars; indeed, it writes its record ineffaceably on the heart which suffers. We really never get over our deep griefs; we are really never altogether the same after we have passed through them as we were before.

"There follows a mist and a weeping rain,
  And life is never the same again."

In one sense, sorrow can never be forgotten. The cares of a long busy life may supervene, but the memory of the first deep sorrows in early youth lives on in perpetual freshness as the little flowers live on beneath the cold snowdrifts through all the long winter. The old woman of ninety remembers her grief and sense of loss seventy years ago, when God took her first baby out of her bosom. We never can actually forget our sorrows, nor is it meant that we should do so. There is a way of remembering grief that is not wrong, that is not a mark of insubmission and that brings rich blessing to our hearts and lives; there is a humanizing and fertilizing influence in sorrow rightly accepted, and "the memory of things precious keepeth warm the heart that once did fold them." Recollections of losses, if sweetened by faith, hope and love, are benedictions to the lives they overshadow. Indeed, they are poor who have never suffered and have none of sorrow's marks upon them; they are poorer far who, having suffered, have forgotten their sufferings and bear in their lives no beautifying traces of the experiences of pain through which they have passed.

> "We turn unblessed from faces fresh with beauty,
>   Unsoftened yet by fears,
> To those whose lines are chased by pain and duty
>   And know the touch of tears.

"The heart whose chords the gentle hand of sadness
    Has touched in minor strain
Is filled with gracious joys, and knows a gladness
    All others seek in vain.

"How poor a life where pathos tells no story,
    Whose pathways reach no shrine,
Which, free from suffering, misses, too, the glory
    Of sympathies divine!"

Yet there is a way of remembering sorrow which brings no blessing, no enrichment—which does not soften the heart nor add beauty to the life. There is an insubmissive remembering which brings no joy, which keeps the heart bitter, which shuts out the sunshine, which broods over losses and trials. Only evil can result from such memory of grief. In a sense, we ought to forget our sorrow. We certainly ought not to stop in the midst of our duties and turn aside and sit down by the graves of our losses, staying there while the tides of busy life sweep on. We should leave our sorrows behind us while we go on reverently, faithfully and quietly in our appointed way.

There are many people, however, who have not learned this lesson; they live perpetually in the shadows of the griefs and losses of their bygone days. Nothing could be more unwholesome or more untrue to the spirit of Christian faith than such a course. **What would** be said or thought of **the man** who should build a house **for** himself **out of** black stones, paint **all the** walls black, hang black **curtains** over the dark-stained windows, put black **carpets** on every floor, festoon the chambers with funereal crape, have only sad pictures on the walls and sad books on the shelves, and should have no lovely plants growing and no sweet flowers blooming anywhere about his home? Would we not look upon such a man with pity as one into whose soul the outer darkness had crept, eclipsing all the beauty of life?

Yet **that is** just the way some people do live. They build for their souls houses just like that; they have memories that let all the bright and joyous things flow away while they retain **all the** sad and bitter things; they forget the pleasant incidents and experiences, the happy hours, the days that came laden with gladness as ships come from distant shores with cargoes of spices; but there has been no painful event in all their life whose memory is not kept ever vivid. They will talk for **hours of** their griefs and bereavements **in** the past, dwelling with a strange morbid pleasure on each sad incident. They keep the old wounds ever unhealed in their hearts; they keep continually in sight pictures and reminiscences of all their lost joys, but none of the joys that are not lost; they forget all their ten thousand blessings in the abiding recollection of the two or three sorrows that have come amid the multitudinous and unremembered joys.

Tennyson's Rizpah says, "The night has crept into my heart, and begun to darken my eyes." So it is with these people who live perpetually in the shadows and glooms of their own sorrows. The darkness creeps into their souls, and all the joyous brightness passes out of their lives, until their very vision becomes so stained that they can no more even discern the glad and lovely colors in God's universe.

Few perversions of life could be sadder than this dwelling ever in the glooms and the shadows of past griefs. It is the will of God that we should turn our eyes away from our sorrows, that we should let the dead past bury its dead, while we go on with reverent earnestness to the new duties and the new joys that await us. By standing and weeping over the grave where it is buried we cannot get back what we have lost. When David's child was dead, he dried his tears and went at once to God's house and worshiped, saying, "Now he is dead, wherefore should I fast? Can I bring him back again? I shall go to him, but he shall not return to me." Instead of weeping over the grave where his dead was not, he turned his eyes forward toward the glory in which his child was waiting for him, and began with new ardor to press toward that home. He turned all the pressure of his grief into the channels of holy living. That is the way every believer in Christ should treat his sorrows. Weeping inconsolably beside a grave can never give back love's vanished treasure. Nor can any blessing come out of such sadness. It does not make the heart any softer; it develops no feature of Christlikeness in the life: it only embitters our present joys and stunts the growth of all beautiful things. The graces of the heart are like flower-plants: they grow well only in the sunshine.

There was a mother who lost by death a lovely daughter. For a long time the mother had been a consistent Christian, but when her child died she refused to be comforted. Her pastor and other Christian friends sought by tender sympathy to draw her thoughts away from her grief, yet all their effort was vain. She would look at nothing but her sorrow; she spent a portion of nearly every day beside the grave where her dead was buried; she would listen to no words of consolation; she would not lift an eye toward the heaven into which her child had gone; she went back no more to the sanctuary, where in the days of her joy she had loved to worship; she shut out of her heart every conception of God's love and kindness and thought of him only as the powerful Being who had torn her sweet child away from her bosom. Thus dwelling in the darkness of inconsolable grief, the joy of her religion left her. Hope's bright visions no longer cheered her, and her heart grew cold and sick with despair. She refused to quit her sorrow and to go on to new joys and toward the glory in which for Christian faith all earth's lost things wait.

There was another mother who also lost a child —one of the rarest and sweetest children that God ever sent to this earth. Never was a heart more completely crushed than was the heart of this bereft mother, yet she did not, like the other woman, sit down in the gloom and dwell there; she did not shut out the sunshine and thrust away the blessing of comfort. She recognized her Father's hand in the grief that had fallen so heavily upon her, and bowed in sweet acquiescence to his will; she opened her heart to the glorious truth of the immortal life, and was comforted **by the simple faith that her** child was with **Christ.** She remembered, too, that she had duties to the living, and turned away from **the** grave where her little one slept in such security, requiring no more any service of earthly affection, to minister to those who still lived and needed her care and love. The result was that her **life** grew richer and more beautiful beneath its baptism **of** sore grief. She came from the deep shadow a lovelier Christian, and her home and a whole community shared the blessing which she had found in her sorrow.

It is easy to see which of these two ways of enduring sorrow is the true one. **We** should forget what we have suffered. The joy set before us should shine upon our souls as the sun shines through clouds, glorifying them. **We** should cherish sacredly and tenderly the memory of our Christian dead, but should train ourselves to think of them as in the home of the blessed with Christ, safely folded, waiting for us. Thus the bright and blessed hopes of immortality should fill us with tranquility and healthy gladness as we move **over the** waves of trial.

"He taketh that we may for ever **keep:**
All that makes life most beautiful and deep,

> Our dearest hopes, by sorrow glorified,
> Beneath his everlasting wings abide;
> For oh, it is our one true need to find
> Earth's vanished bliss in heavenly glory shrined."

We should remember that the blessings which have gone away are not all that God has for us. This summer's flowers will all fade by and by when winter's cold breath smites them—we shall not be able to find one of them in the fields or gardens during the long, cold, dreary months to come—yet we shall know all the while that God has other flowers preparing, just as fragrant and as lovely as those which have perished. Spring will come again, and under its warm breath the earth will be covered once more with floral beauty as rich as that which faded in the autumn. So the joys that have gone from our homes and our hearts are not the only joys; God has others in store just as rich as those we have lost, and in due time he will give us these to fill our emptied hands.

One of the worst dangers of inconsolable sorrow is that it may lead us to neglect our duty to the living in our mourning for the dead. This we should never do. God does not desire us to give up our work because our hearts are broken. We may not even pause long with our sorrows; we may not sit down beside the graves of our dead and linger there, cherishing our grief. "**Let** the dead bury their dead," said the Master to one who wished to bury his father and then follow him; "but come **thou** and follow me." Not even the tender offices of love might detain him who was called to the higher service. The lesson is for all, and for all **time.** Duty ever presses, and we have scarcely laid our dead away out of our sight before its **earnest** calls that will not be denied are sounding in our ears.

A distinguished general related this pathetic incident of his own experience in our civil war. **The** general's son was a lieutenant of battery. An assault was in progress. The father was leading his division in a charge; as he pressed on in the field suddenly his eye was caught by the sight of a dead battery-officer lying just before him. One glance showed him it was his own son. His fatherly impulse was to stop beside the dear form and give vent to his grief, but the duty of the moment demanded that he should press on **in** the charge; so, quickly snatching one hot kiss from the dead lips, he hastened away, leading his command in the assault.

Ordinarily the pressure is not so intense, and we can pause longer to weep and do honor to the memory of our dead. Yet in all sorrow the principle is

THE DUTY OF FORGETTING SORROW.

the same. God does not desire us to waste our life in tears. We are to put our grief into new energy of service. Sorrow should make us more reverent, more earnest, more useful. God's work should never be allowed to suffer while we stop to weep. The fires must still be kept burning on the altar, and the worship must go on. The work in the household, in the school, in the store, in the field, must be taken up again—the sooner, the better. Ofttimes, indeed, the death of one in the circle is a divine voice calling the living to new duty. Thus, when a father dies, the mother is ordained to double responsibility; if there is a son of thoughtful age, his duty is not bitter grieving, but prompt taking up of the work that has fallen from the father's dead hands. When our friends are taken from us, our bereavement is a call, not to bitter weeping, but to new duty.

> "It bids us do the work that they laid down—
>   Take up the song where they broke off the strain;
> So journeying till we reach the heavenly town
>   Where are laid up our treasures and our crown,
>   And our lost loved ones will be found again."

Sometimes it is care only that is laid down when death comes, as when a mother puts her baby away into the grave; no work drops out of the little hands for the mother to take up. But may we not then say that, since God has emptied her hands of their own care and duty, he has some other work for them to do? He has set them **free** from their own tasks that with their trained skill and their enriched sympathies **they may** serve others.

In a sick-room there was a little rosebush in a **pot in** the window. There was only one rose on the bush, and its face was turned full toward the light. This fact was noticed and spoken of, when one said that the rose would look no other way but toward the light. Experiments had been made with it; it had been turned away from the window, its face toward the gloom of the interior, but in a little time it would resume its old position. With wonderful persistence it refused to face the darkness and insisted on ever looking toward the light.

The flower has its lesson for **us. We should** never allow ourselves to face toward life's glooms; we should never sit down **in** the shadows of **any** sorrow and let the night darken over us **into the gloom of** despair; **we** should **turn our faces away toward the** light and quicken every energy **for braver duty** and truer, holier service. **Grief** should always make us better and give us new skill and power; it should make our hearts softer, our spirits kindlier, our touch more gentle; it should teach us its holy lessons, and we should learn them, and then go on with sorrow's sacred ordination upon us to new love and better service.

It is thus, too, that lonely hearts find their sweetest, richest comfort. Sitting down to brood over our sorrows, the darkness deepens about us and our little strength changes to weakness; but if we turn away from the gloom and take up the tasks of comforting and helping others, the light will come again and we shall grow strong.

> " When all our hopes are gone,
> 'Tis well our hands must still keep toiling on
> For others' sake;
> For strength to bear is found in duty done,
> And he is blest indeed who learns to make
> The joy of others cure his own heartache."

XVIII.

PEOPLE WHO FAIL.

> "Not many lives, but only one, have we—
> One, only one.
> How sacred that one life should ever be,
> That narrow span,
> Day after day filled up with blessed toil,
> Hour after hour still bringing in new spoil!"
>
> BONAR.

THERE are many people who fail. Yet there are two standards by which success and failure may be measured: there is the world's standard, and there is God's. Many whom men set down as having failed are successful in the higher sense, while many of earth's vaunted successes are really complete and terrible failures.

If we are wise, we will seek to know life's realities, and will not be fooled by its appearances. True success must be something which will not perish in earth's wreck or decay, something which will not be torn out of our hands in the hour of death, something which will last over into the eternal years. No folly can be so great as that which gives all life's energies to the building up of something, however beautiful it may be, which must soon be torn down, and which cannot possibly be carried beyond the grave.

The real failures in life are not those which are registered in commercial agencies and reported as bankruptcies, nor those whose marks are the decay of earthly fortune, descent in the social scale, the breaking down of worldly prosperity, or any of those signs by which men rate one another. A man may fail in these ways, and, as Heaven sees him, his path may be like the shining light, growing in brightness all the time. His heart may remain pure and his hands clean through all his earthly misfortunes. He may be growing all the while in the elements of true manhood. In the autumn days the stripping off of the leaves uncovers the nests of the birds; and for many a man the stripping away of the leaves of earthly prosperity is the disclosing to him of the soul's true nest and home in the bosom of God. We cannot call that life a failure which, though losing money and outward show, is itself growing every day nobler, stronger, Christlier. It matters little what becomes of one's circumstances if meanwhile the man himself is prospering. Circumstances are but the scaffolding amid which the building rises.

The real failures are those whose marks are in the life itself and in the character. A man prospers in the world. He grows rich. He gathers luxuries and the appointments of wealth about him instead of the plain circumstances amid which he spent his early days. The cottage is exchanged for a mansion; he is a millionaire; he has wide influence; men wait at his door to ask favors of him; he is sought and courted by the great; his name is everywhere known. But the heart which nestled in purity under the home-made jacket has not retained its purity under rich broadcloth: it has become the home of pride, ambition, unrest, unholy schemes, and of much that is corrupt and evil; his knee bends no more in prayer as in childhood it was taught to bend at a mother's knee; his life is stained with many sins; his character has lost its former innocence and loveliness. His circumstances have advanced from poverty to wealth, but the man himself dwelling within the circle of the circumstances has deteriorated. What could be sadder than the following picture?—

"Where is the promise of the years
Once written on my brow,

Ere errors, agonies and fears
Brought with **them all** that speaks **in tears**—
Ere I had **sunk** beneath my peers?
   Where sleeps that promise now?

" Naught lingers **to** redeem those **hours**
   Still, still to memory sweet;
The flowers that bloom **in sunny bowers**
Are withered all, and **evil** towers
Supreme above her sister-powers
   Of sorrow and deceit.

" **I look along** the columned **years**
   And see life's **riven fane**
Just where it fell amid the jeers
Of scornful lips whose mocking sneers
For ever hiss within mine ears
   To break the sleep of pain.

" I can but own my life **is** vain—
   A desert **void of** peace.
I missed the **goal** I sought to gain,
I missed the measure of the strain
That lulls fame's **fever** in the brain
   And bids **earth's** tumult cease.

" **Myself!** Alas for theme so poor—
   A **theme but rich** in fear!
I stand **a** wreck on error's shore,
A spectre not within **the door,**
A homeless shadow evermore,
   An exile lingering here."

There is a story of **a man who built his enemy into the wall** of the castle he was erecting—made a tomb for him there, and buried him alive in the heart of the magnificent pile he was setting up. That is what many men do with their souls in their earthly prosperity: they bury them in the heart of their successes. It is a splendid monument which they rear; but when it is finished it is the mausoleum of their manhood. Shall we call that true success which erects a pile of earthly grandeur to dazzle men's eyes while it strangles a man's spiritual life and forfeits him the divine favor and a home in heaven?

There is no doubt that God creates every human soul for a high destiny; he has a plan for every life, and that plan in every case is noble and beautiful. There is no blind fate which predestines any soul to failure and perdition. No man is born in this world who may not make his life a true success and attain at last to coronation in heaven. Every soul is endowed at creation for a noble career. It may not be for a brilliant career, with honor and fame and great power; but there is no one born who is not so gifted that with his endowments he may fill his own place and do his allotted work. And there can be no nobleness higher than this. Then to every one come the opportunities by which he may achieve the success for which he was born. No man can ever say he had no chance to be noble; the trouble is with the man himself. Opportunities offer, but he does not embrace them, and while he delays they pass on and away, to return no more; for "lost chance comes not again." Opportunities are doors opened to beauty and blessing, but they are not held open for laggards, and in a moment they are shut, never to be opened again.

Both in original endowments and in opportunities every life is furnished for success. "But men are weak and sinful, and are unable to make their lives noble." True, but here comes in the blessed secret of divine help. No one need ever fail, for God is with men—with every one who does not thrust him away—and he is ready to put his own strength under human infirmity, so that the weakest may overcome and rise into beauty and strength. No man is foredoomed to failure; there is no man who may not make his life a true success. Those who fail, fail because they will not build their life after the pattern shown them in the mount, because they do not use the endowments which God has bestowed upon them, because they reject the opportunities offered to them, or because they leave God out of their life and enter the battle only in their own strength.

The saddest thing **in this world** is the wreck of a life made for God and for immortality, but failing of all the high ends of its existence and lying **in ruin** at the last, when it is too late to begin anew. The poet's lines portray this sadness **in vivid colors:**

"Upon the hour when I was born
    God said, 'Another man shall **be;'**
And the great Maker did not scorn
    Out of himself to fashion me.
He sunned me with his ripening looks,
    And heaven's rich instincts in me grew
As effortless **as** woodland nooks
    Send violets up and paint them blue.

"Men think it is an awful sight
    To see a soul just set adrift
On that drear voyage from whose night
    The ominous shadows never lift;
But 'tis more awful to behold
    A helpless infant newly born,
Whose little hands unconscious hold
    The keys of darkness and of morn.

"**Mine** held them once; I flung away
    Those keys that might have open set
The golden sluices of the day,
    But clutch the keys of darkness yet.
I hear the reapers singing go
    Into **God's** harvest; I, that might
With them have chosen, here below
    Grope shuddering at the gates of night.

> "O glorious youth, that once wast mine!
>   O high ideal! all in vain
> Ye enter at this ruined shrine
>   Whence worship ne'er shall rise again;
> The bat and owl inhabit here,
>   The snake nests in the altar-stone,
> The sacred vessels moulder near,
>   The image of the God is gone."

To the readers of this book this chapter is cautionary. The paths that lead to failure begin far back and slope down, usually in very gradual and almost imperceptible decline, toward the fatal end. The work of the Christian teacher is not with those who have hopelessly failed, wrecked all and gone down into the dark waters—these are beyond his warning voice and his helping hand—but he should seek in time to save from failure those whose faces are just turning toward its sunless blackness.

It may be that these words shall come to one whose feet are already set in paths of peril. There are many such paths, and so disguised are they by the enemy of men's souls that ofttimes to the unwary they appear harmless. They are flower-strewn. They begin at first in very slight and in only momentary deviations from the narrow path of duty and of safety. Young people should be honest with themselves in these matters. The question at first is not, "What are you doing now?" but, "Which way are you facing? What are the **tendencies of your life?**" **If** the compass register falsely by but a hair's breadth when the ship puts out to sea, it will carry her a thousand miles out of her course a few days hence, and may wreck her. The slightest wrong tendency of life **in early youth**, unless corrected, will lead at length far away from God and from hope. Montaigne says:

> "Habit at first is but a silken thread,
> Fine as the light-winged gossamers that sway
> In the warm sunbeams of a summer's day;
>   A shallow streamlet rippling o'er its bed;
>   **A** tiny sapling ere its roots are spread;
> **A** yet-unhardened **thorn** upon the spray;
> A lion's whelp that hath not scented prey;
>   A little smiling child obedient led.
> Beware! That thread may bind thee as a chain;
>   That streamlet gather to a fatal **sea**;
>   That sapling spread into a gnarlèd tree;
> That thorn, grown hard, may wound and give thee pain;
>   That playful whelp his murderous fangs reveal;
>   That child, a giant, crush thee 'neath his heel."

We should always deal frankly with ourselves. We must not fancy that we are so different from other people that what is perilous for them is yet safe enough for us. It is a sacred and most momentous responsibility which is put into our hand when our life is entrusted to us. Life is God's most wonderful gift. Then, it is not our own, to do with as we please. It belongs to God and is but a trust in our hands, as when one puts into the hand of another a precious gem or some other costly and valuable possession to be carried amid dangers and delivered in safety at the end of the journey.

God has given us our life, and there are two things which he requires us to do with it. First, we are to keep it. Enemies will assail us and try to wrest from us the sacred jewel, but we are to guard and defend it at whatever cost. Then, mere keeping is not all of our obligation. The man with the one talent seems to have kept the talent safely enough: he wrapped it up and laid it away in a secure place. It did not gather rust; no one robbed him of it. When his master returned he presented it to him safe and unspotted. But he had done only part of his duty, and was condemned because he had not used his talent and thereby increased its value. The lesson is plain. It is not enough to guard our soul from stain and from robbery: we must also make such use of it as shall bless the world and develop our life itself into ripeness of beauty and of power. Our endowments come to us only as possibilities, powers folded up in buds or germs which we must draw out by use and culture. **We are responsible** not merely for guarding and keeping the possibilities which God **puts** into our **lives,** but also for developing these possibilities until the **talents** multiply into many, until the little seeds grow into strong and fruitful plants or trees.

There are, then, two lines of possible failure. **We** may not guard our life from the **world's** corrupting **influence,** nor defend it from the enemies that would **filch** from us the precious jewel. All who yield to temptations and fall into sin's slavery fail in this way. Then, we may neglect to make the most of our life, developing its possibilities, cultivating it to its highest capacities for beauty and using it to **its last** degree of power in doing good. Thus indolence leads to failure. **A** young person who has good mental powers and is too slothful and inert to study and thus educate, or draw out, the possibilities of **his** endowment, is failing in life **just so far as** his indolence **is** leaving his talent buried in his brain. The same is true of all the capacities **of** life. The lazy man is a failure. **He** may be richly gifted and may have the largest **and** best opportunities, but he has no energy to do the work that comes to his **hand;** then, while he **lingers,** indolent and self-indulgent, the opportunities pass on and pass away, to return no more, and the powers of his being meanwhile die within him. He comes to the end of his life without having left in the world any worthy record of his existence, anything to show that he ever lived, and with only a shriveled soul to carry up to God's bar.

No other curses in the Bible are more bitter than those upon uselessness. A man made for a great mission, and magnificently endowed for it, who does nothing with his life, even though he do not yield to sin and turn the forces of his being into courses of evil, is still a terrible failure. Uselessness is failure. The penalty upon such malfeasance in duty is loss of unused capacities, the wasting and shriveling of the powers which might have been developed to such grandeur and trained to such efficiency and influence. The eye unused loses its power to see; the tongue unused becomes dumb; the heart unused grows cold and hard; the brain unused withers to imbecility.

To save our lives, then, from at least some degree of failure, it is necessary that we not only keep ourselves unspotted from the world, but also that we make the fullest possible use of all the powers God has given us. Hence every young person who would save his life from failure must begin with the bright, golden days now passing, and make each one of them beautiful with the beauty of fidelity and earnestness. A wasted youth is a bad beginning for a successful life. We have not a moment to lose, for the time allotted to us is not an instant too long for the tasks and duties which God has set for us.

We shall have no second chance if we fail in our first. Some things we may do over if we fail in our first or second attempt, but we can live our life only once. To fail in our first probation is to lose all.

> "'Tis not for man to trifle: life is brief,
>   And sin is here;
> Our age is but the falling of a leaf,
>   A dropping tear.
> We have no time to sport away the hours;
> All must be earnest in a world like ours."

XIX.

LIVING VICTORIOUSLY.

"The cross for only a day,
  The crown for ever and aye—
The one for a night that will soon be gone,
The one for eternity's glorious morn.

"The cross—that I'll cheerfully bear,
  Nor sorrow for loss or care;
For a moment only the pain and the strife,
But through endless ages the crown of life."

LIFE is conflict. Every good thing lies beyond a battlefield, and we must fight our way to it. There must be struggle to get it. This is true in physical life; from infancy to old age existence is a fight with infirmity and disease. In mental life the same is true. Education is a long conflict; the powers of the mind have to fight their way to strength and development. So it is in spiritual life; enemies throng the path and contest every step of progress. No one ever attains to beauty and nobleness of character save through long and sore struggle.

Many of earth's great historic battlefields are now spots of quiet peace. Once men met there in deadly strife—arms clashed, cannon thundered, the air was filled with the shouts of contending armies and the groans of the wounded and dying, and the ground was covered with the dead—but now, in summer days, the grass waves on the once bloody field, sweet flowers bloom, harvests yellow to ripeness, children play and the air is full of bird-songs and the voices of peace. But he who walks over the spot is continually reminded of the terrible struggle which occurred there in the bygone days.

We look upon men and women who have attained high culture of mind and spirit. They are intelligent and educated; they are well balanced in their faculties and symmetrical in their development; their character is strong and noble, showing all the features which belong to true manhood or true womanhood; they are dignified in their deportment, calm and equable in their bearing; they are not hasty in speech nor impetuous in temper; their judgments are never rash; they possess the qualities of patience, contentment and gentleness, combined with courage, righteousness and strength. When we look upon such people, we cannot but admire them and be fascinated by the culture and the majesty and serenity of their lives. We are apt to think of them as highly favored in their original endowment and in their circumstances and experiences.

But if we knew the story of these lives, we should see that where now we behold such ripe and beautiful character was once a battlefield. These men and women began just as all of us must begin—with their faculties undeveloped, their powers undisciplined and their lives uncultured. They had their hard battles with evil in themselves and with evil about them; they grew into intelligence through long and severe mental training and years of diligent study; they attained their splendid self-control through painful experiences of conflict with their tongues, their tempers, their original impetuosity, their many innate propensities to evil; their beauty of Christian character they reached through the submission of their own wills to the will of Christ and of their selfishness and natural resentment and other evil affections and passions to the sway of the spirit of divine love. They were not always what now they are. This noble beauty which we so admire is the fruit of long years of sore struggle, the harvest which has been brought to ripeness by the frosts of autumn, the snows and storms of winter and the rains and sunshine of spring. Back of the calmness, the refinement, the strength and the charming culture which we see is a story of conflict, with many a defeat and many a wounding, and of stern self-discipline, with pain, toil and tears.

We all admire the character of Saint John as it is drawn for us in the New Testament. It seems almost perfect in its affectionateness, its gentleness, its peacefulness. Yet John was not always the saintly man of the Gospel. There is no doubt that he attained this beauty of character, under the transforming influence of Christ's love, through just such sore conflict and self-discipline as all of us must endure to attain Christlikeness. A writer compares the character of this man of love to an extinct volcano he had visited. Where once the crater yawned there is now a verdurous cuplike hollow on the mountain-summit; where once the fierce fires had burned lies now a still, clear pool of water, looking up like an eye to the beautiful heavens above, its banks covered with sweet flowers. Says Dr. Culross, speaking of the beloved apostle and referring to this old crater now so beautiful, "It is an apt parable of this man. Naturally and originally volcanic, capable of profoundest passion and daring, he is new-made by grace, till in his old age he stands out in calm grandeur of character and depth and largeness of soul, with all the gentlenesses and graces of Christ adorning him—a man, as I image him to myself, with a face so noble that kings might do him homage, and so sweet that children would run to him for his blessing."

So we learn the story of all noble, cultured character. It is reached only through struggle; it is not natural, but is the fruit of toil and conquest; it bears the marks and scars of many a conflict. We often hear people say they would give large sums to have such a person's contentment, or self-control, or sweetness of disposition, or submissiveness to God's will, or power of giving sympathy. These are things that cannot be bought, and that cannot be learned in any school. Such qualities can be gotten only through victorious struggle during years of experience.

We say that Christ gives his disciples this spiritual loveliness, that he renews their natures and transforms their lives, imprinting his own image upon them. This is true; if it were not, there could never be any hope of saintliness in any human life. Yet Christ does not produce this change in us merely by instantaneously printing his likeness upon our souls as the photographer prints one's picture on the glass in his camera. He works in us, but we must work out the beauty which he puts in germ into our hearts; he helps us in every struggle, yet still we must struggle; he never fights the battle for us, although he is ever near to help us. Thus the noble things of spiritual attainment lie away beyond the hills and the rivers, and we must toil far through strife and pain before we can get them. The old life must be crucified that the new life may emerge. George MacDonald has put this lesson in quaint yet striking way in one of his poems:

> " ' Traveler, what lies over the hill?
>   Traveler, tell to me;
>   I am only a child: from the window-sill
>   Over I cannot see.'
>
> " ' Child, there's a valley over there,
>   Pretty and woody and shy,
>   And a little brook that says, "Take care,
>   Or I'll drown you by and by." '
>
> " ' And what comes next?'—'A lonely moor
>   Without a beaten way,
>   And gray clouds sailing slow before
>   A wind that will not stay.'

"'And then?'—'Dark rocks and yellow sand,
    And a moaning sea beside.'—
'And then?'—'More sea, more sea, more land,
    And rivers deep and wide.'

"'And then?'—'Oh, rock and mountain and vale,
    Rivers and fields and men,
Over and over—a weary tale—
    And round to your home again.'

"'Is that the end? It is weary at best.'—
    'No, child; it is not the end.
On summer eves, away in the west,
    You will see a stair ascend,

"'Built of all colors of lovely stones—
    A stair up into the sky,
Where no one is weary, and no one moans
    Or wishes to be laid by.'

"'I will go!'—'But the steps are very steep;
    If you would climb up there,
You must lie at its foot, as still as sleep,
    And be a step of the stair

"'For others to put their feet on you
    To reach the stones high-piled,
Till Jesus comes and takes you too,
    And leads you up, my child.'"

The duty of life is, then, to be victorious. Every good thing, every noble thing, must be won. Heaven is for those who overcome; not to overcome is to fail. In war, to be defeated is to become a slave. To be vanquished in the battle with sin is to become sin's slave; to be overcome by the antagonisms of life is to lose all. But in the Christian life defeat is never a necessity. Over all the ills and enmities of this world we may be victorious.

Moreover, every Christian life *ought* to be victorious. Jesus said, "In the world ye shall have tribulation: but be of good cheer; I have overcome the world." Nothing will do for a gospel for sinners which leaves any enmity unconquered, any foe unvanquished. Saint Paul, in speaking of the trials and sufferings that beset the Christian—tribulation, distress, persecution, famine, nakedness, sword—asked, "Shall these separate us from the love of Christ?" That is, "Can these evils and antagonisms ever be so great that we cannot overcome them and be carried still in Christ's bosom?" He answers his own question by saying triumphantly, "Nay, in all these things we are more than conquerors through Him that loved us." We need never be defeated; we may always be victorious. We may be even "more than conquerors"—triumphant, exultant conquerors. "Whatsoever is born of God overcometh the world; and this is the victory that overcometh the world, even our faith."

The ideal Christian life is one, therefore, which is victorious over all enmity, opposition, difficulty and suffering. This is the standard which we should all set for ourselves; this is the pattern shown us in the holy mount after which we should seek always to fashion our life. We need never expect to find a path running along on a level plain, amid sweet flowers, beneath the shade of the trees.

> "'Does the road wind up hill all the way?'—
> 'Yes, to the end.'—
> 'Will the day's journey take the whole long day?'—
> 'From morn to night, my friend.'"

Of course there will be Elims in the long way, for God is very loving, but the road will always be steep and hard. Yet there will never come an experience in which it will not be wrong for us to be defeated. Grace has lost none of its power since New-Testament days. Surely the poor stumbling life so many of us live is not the best possible living for us if we are true Christians. Our Master is able to help us to something far better.

Take temper, the control of the emotion of anger, the government of the tongue. Is there any real reason, any fatal necessity, why we should always be easily provoked, swept away by every slight cause into unseemly passion and into unchristian speech? No doubt Scripture is true to experience when it affirms that the taming of the tongue is harder than the taming **of any** kind of beast or bird or serpent. No doubt the control of the tongue is the hardest victory **to** be achieved in all the range of self-discipline, for inspiration affirms that the man who has gotten the complete victory over his speech is a perfectly disciplined man, "able also to bridle **the** whole body." Yet victory **even** here is not impossible. The grace **of** God is sufficient to enable us to live sweetly **amid all** provocation and irritation, **to** check **all** feelings of resentment, to give the soft answer which will turn away wrath, and to choke back all rising bitterness before it shall break into **a** storm of passion. Jesus never lost his temper **nor** spoke unadvisedly, and he is able to help us to live in the same victorious way.

This is the ideal life for a child of God. We may be more than conquerors. It is not an easy conquest that we may win in a day; in many lives **it must** be the work of **years.** Still, it is possible, with Christ to help; and we should never relax our diligence nor withdraw from the battle until we are victorious. He who in the strength of Christ has acquired this power of self-control has reached a sublime rank in spiritual culture. The world may sneer at the man who bears injury and wrong without resentment, without anger, but in God's eyes he is a spiritual hero.

> "Call no man weak who can a grievance brook
>   And hold his peace against a red-hot word,
> Nor him a coward who averts his look
>   For fear some sleeping passion may be stirred.
>
> "But call him weak who tramples not in dust
>   Those evil things that fascinate the heart;
> Who fears to give his moral foe a thrust
>   And springs from duty with a coward start;
>
> "Who grapples not with one defiant sin;
>   Whose ease and pride and pleasure keep the post.
> Where self is strong, weakest passions win;
>   Where self is weakest—there, the valiant host."

Take trial of any kind—pain, misfortune, sorrow. Is it possible to live victoriously at this point of human experience? Many fail to do so; they succumb to every trial and are overwhelmed by every wave of grief or loss. Many do not make any effort to resist; the faith of their creed, of their hymns, of their prayers, forsakes them, and they meet their troubles apparently as unsupported and unsustained as if they were not Christians at all. A novelist describes one in grief as he stands on the shore and gazes at the ship that is bearing away from him the **object** of his heart's devotion. In his absorbing anguish he does not observe that **the** tide is rising. It rolls over **his feet,** but he **is** unconscious of it. Higher and higher the waters rise—now to his knees, now to his loins, now to his breast. But all his thought is **on** the receding ship, and he **is oblivious** to **the** swelling of the waves, and at length they **flow over** his head and he is swept down to death. **This is** a picture **of** many of earth's **sufferers in** sorrow or in misfortune. They are defeated and overborne **; the** divine promises do not sustain them, because they lose all faith ; they hear the words, " **Ye** sorrow not, even as others which have no hope," and yet they do sorrow just as if they had no hope.

But this is not the best that our religion can do **for** us. **It** is designed **to** give us complete victory in all trial. **"As** sorrowing yet always rejoicing" **is** the scriptural ideal for a Christian life. Christ has bequeathed his own peace to his believing ones. We know what his peace was ; it was never broken for a moment, though his sorrows and sufferings surpassed in bitterness anything this earth has ever known in any other sufferer. The same peace he **offers to each** one of his people in all trial.

The artist painted life as a sea, wild, swept **by**

storms, covered with wrecks. In the midst of this troubled scene he painted a great rock rising out of the waves, and in the rock, above the reach of the billows, a cleft with herbage growing and flowers blooming, and in the midst of the herbage and the flowers a dove sitting quietly on her nest. It is a picture of the Christian's heritage of peace in tribulation. It is thus Christ would have us live in the world—in the midst of the sorest trials and adversities always victorious, always at peace. The secret of this victoriousness is faith—faith in the unchanging love of God, faith in the unfailing grace and help of Christ, faith in the immutable divine promises. If we but believe God and go forward ever resolute and unfaltering in duty, we shall always be more than conquerors.

XX.
SHUT IN.

> "A little bird I am,
> Shut from the fields of air,
> And in my cage I sit and sing
> To Him who placed me there,
> Well pleased a prisoner to be
> Because, my God, it pleases thee."
>
> MADAME GUYON.

IN a midsummer business-letter to a lady whose pen writes many bright things for children's papers the writer, not knowing of her invalidism, expressed the hope that his correspondent might be enjoying a pleasant and restful vacation. In the allusion to this wish, in her reply, there was a touching pathos, though there was not a word of complaint. She wrote: "I am always an invalid, and my outing consists only in lying down in another place." She is one of the Lord's prisoners. Yet there is no gloom in her prison; her faith fills it with brightness. It is a chamber of peace; the voice of song is heard in it. Her "outing consists only in lying down in another place," but always the Lord her Shepherd makes her "to lie down in green pastures." Nor is she cut off from the joy of serving Christ, but is permitted in her quiet sanctuary to do many beautiful things for him, blessing many a life out in the sunshine by her loving ministry within her doors. She can sing again with Madame Guyon,

> "My cage confines me round:
>   Abroad I cannot fly;
> But, though my wing is closely bound,
>   My heart's at liberty.
> My prison-walls cannot control
> The flight, the freedom, of my soul."

There are many people who belong to the "shut-ins." They are found in fine city mansions and in quiet country homes, in the dwellings of the rich and in the cottages of the poor. They are invalids who because of their broken health cannot any longer run the race with the swift or fight the battle with the strong; they have been wounded in the strife, and have fallen out of the ranks. Passers-by on the street sometimes see their faces at the window, white and bearing marks of suffering, but they no longer mingle with the hurrying throngs nor take their places with the busy toilers. They are "shut in."

They represent many degrees of invalidism. Some of them are almost entirely helpless. **Here** is one who for many years has not lifted a hand nor moved a finger by her own volition; here is **one** only partially powerless, unable to walk, but having the use of hands and arms; another has **not** sufficient strength for any active out-door duty, but **can** move about the house and perform many a sweet ministry of love. Thus these "shut-ins" **embrace** all degrees of suffering and of helplessness, but they are alike in their inability to join **the** ranks **of** the busy workers without. They must stay in-doors; in **a** sense, they are prisoners in this great bright world, no longer free to **go** where they **would or** to do what they earnestly crave to do.

This book may find its way into the hands of some of these "shut-ins," and it ought to have its message for them. The message ought also to be one of cheer and gladness. I would like to write for **such** "prisoners of the Lord" a word that may carry comfort and strength, that may be to them **like a** little flower sent in from the outside, **a** token of sympathy laden also with fragrance from **the** garden of the Lord.

In **the** account of the entering of Noah into the

ark, before the Flood came, we read that "the Lord shut him in." For quite a year Noah and his family were "shut-ins," but it must have been a comfort for them to know that the shutting of the door was not accidental—that the Lord had done it. There was another comfort: it was very much better inside than outside. Without, there were great storms, wild torrents and terrible destruction. No man could live in the rushing waters. Within, there was perfect safety. Not a drop of rain dashed in; no wild tempest swept through the door. The ark was a chamber of peace floating quietly and securely in the midst of the most terrible ruin the world ever saw. The Lord's shutting in of his people was to save them.

May we not say of every shut-in child of God, "The Lord shut him in"? What the Lord does for his own people can never be unkindness, whatever it may seem to be. It is an infinite comfort, therefore, to a Christian who is kept within-doors by invalidism or other like cause to be able to say, "It was the Lord who shut me in."

May we not go a step farther and say of such "shut-ins" that the Lord has shut them in because it is better for them to be within than without? No doubt there is protection in such a condition.

15

These prisoners of the Lord are not exposed to the storms; it is always warm and safe where they are. They are dwelling under the shadow of God's wing. They miss many of the struggles with temptation and many of the sterner conflicts of life by being shut in. The ark was guided by an unseen Hand over the trackless waters of the Deluge. It had no rudder, no pilot, no sail, no chart, yet it struck no rock, was whelmed in no wild billows, moved in no wrong course, and bore its "shut-ins" in safety to the shores of a new world. May we not say that in like manner all the "shut-ins" of God's people are God's peculiar care? Are they not of those whom he gathers in his arms and carries in his bosom? We are told that the Lord knoweth how to deliver the godly out of temptation; may we not say that one of the ways he delivers from temptation is by shutting his people away from the rough blasts? No doubt many a soul has been saved from the evil influences of worldliness by being called from the midst of the excitements and strifes of active life into the quiet shelter of invalidism. The chamber of suffering proves a sanctuary rather than a prison.

But there are other comforts. It is a great deal better to be shut in than to be shut out. There are pictures of both classes in the New Testament. In one of the parables of our Lord the door was shut, and it excluded some who came too late to be admitted; but the same door also shut in with Christ those who had entered in time. No condition could be more suggestive of blessedness than to be shut in with the Master. The closed doors are pledge that there can be no interruption of the communion. Christ's "shut-ins" have abundant opportunity for loving fellowship with him. Their sick-rooms are not prisons, but Bethels where Christ comes to meet with them and to bless them.

It is not strange, therefore, that many of the quiet rooms where Christ's disciples are shut in are places of great joy. Faith triumphs over pain. The darkness brings out the stars of promise, and they shine in radiant beauty. Because of infirmity the power of Christ rests in especial measure upon his suffering ones, and they are enabled to rejoice in their very tribulations. Their joy is rich and deep. It is not the rippling surface-happiness of those outside who have no pain and are free to go where they will and to do as they desire: it is heart-joy which does not depend upon external things, and is therefore unaffected by external experiences. There are fresh-water springs that bubble up beneath the edge of the sea; the brackish tides roll over them, but they remain ever sweet and fresh. Like these springs are the fountains of Christian joy. Under the billows of trial and suffering they flow on unwasting and unembittered. Many Christian invalids become almost marvels of patience and peace as they **are** brought into living communion with Christ. They are never heard complaining; they believe in the love of God, submit themselves to his will, and take pain **from** his hand as confidently and sweetly as they take medicine from their trusted physicians; their faces **shine with** the radiance of indwelling peace, and the joy of their hearts finds expression in **words** and songs of praise. Surely, to the angels, as they look down from their pure glory, the chambers in which many of Christ's "shut-ins" **lie must** appear as spots of bright beauty in this **dark** world.

> "Shut in by o'ermastering weakness
> From the world's ceaseless bustle and din—
> From sanctified, diligent purpose
> And noble endeavor shut in;
> But never shut in from the spirit
> Of meekness, contentment and love
> That gathers and fashions life's jewels
> For chaplets of glory above.

"Shut in, but the Spirit commissioned
　The purpose divine to unfold
Has graciously circled each letter
　With halos of ruby and gold.
Wherever the sunshine of patience
　Is peacefully shining within
The pencil of beauty seraphic
　Has written, in mercy, 'Shut in.'"

We naturally suppose that when persons are laid aside by illness and shut away in quiet sick-rooms their work ceases and their usefulness is at an end. After that they are a burden to others instead of being helpers. So we would say. They require tending, watching, nursing; probably they have to be lifted by their friends and carried from chair to bed, from room to room, up and down stairs; they can no longer take any part in the duty of the household nor perform any active service for the Master. We would say at first thought that they are no longer useful; their old-time work has dropped from their hands, and others now have to do it. Yet we greatly mistake when we suppose they are no longer of any service: they have a ministry even in their suffering which in many cases exceeds in value their highest usefulness in their most active days. It is impossible to measure the influence in a home, day after day, of a patient, **rejoicing** Christian sufferer. There pours out from the sick-room of such a "shut-in" a spiritual warmth of love which diffuses itself through all the household life like a summer atmosphere, leaving benediction everywhere.

It was my privilege to visit very often a Christian young woman who for years was a sufferer. Much of the time her pain was excruciating—almost unendurable; but as I watched her from week to week I saw continually the putting forth of new spiritual beauties in her character. Her young life seemed to me **like a** lovely rose-bush in early summer with its many opening buds, and pain was as the summer warmth that caused the buds to burst into full, rich beauty and fragrance. Every time I saw her some new feature of Christlikeness appeared in her life: another rose had opened into full bloom. In her last months there was no opportunity for active service, yet I believe the good she wrought by her ministry of pain far surpassed that which she could have done in the same time with the busiest hands had she lived in painless health. By her suffering she touched the hearts of parents and friends and drew out their sympathy as they watched month after month beside her. These fruits of her pain will remain as permanent enrichment of the **characters of those who loved** her. Another effect of **her** suffering was in the influence of her sweet patience. **She** never murmured; **her** faith was never clouded for an instant; she was gentle, thoughtful, joyous, even in the **sorest** pain. Thus she was preaching perpetually sermons without words on the power of the love and grace of God, and thus became a blessing **to every** one who entered her **room and looked** upon her radiant face.

From very humble life there comes this pathetic incident **which** illustrates the same truth: **In a** pottery there was a workman who had one small invalid child at home. The man wrought **at his** trade with exemplary fidelity. **He** managed, however, **to** bear each evening to the **bedside** of his "wee lad" a flower, a **bit of** ribbon **or a fragment** of crimson glass—anything that would lie on the white counterpane and give color to the room. He never went home at night without something that would make the **wan face** light up with joy at his return. He never said that he loved his boy, and yet he went on patiently loving him until the whole shop had been drawn into real though unconscious fellowship with him. The workmen made curious little jars and cups, and painted diminutive pictures on them, and burnt them in their kilns. **One** brought some fruit and another some engravings **in a scrapbook.** Not one of them whispered **a** word, for this solemn thing was not to be talked about. They put their little gifts in the old man's hat, and he found them there and understood it **all.** The entire pottery-full of men of rather coarse fibre by nature grew quiet as the months passed, becoming gentle and kind; some dropped swearing as the weary look **on** their patient fellow-worker's **face** told them beyond mistake that the inevitable shadow was drawing nearer.

Every day some one did a piece **of** work for him, so that he could come later and go earlier. **And** when the bell tolled and the little coffin came out of the lonely door, there stood a hundred stalwart workingmen from the pottery with their clean clothes on, losing their half-day's time from work for the privilege of following to the grave that little child whom probably **not** one of them **had** ever seen.

These incidents illustrate the refining, softening influence that went out from even **a** child's sick-room and touched a hundred men. **All** over the country there are other chambers of suffering from which there goes out continually **a power** that makes men and and women quieter, gentler, more thoughtful and kind. Thus God's "shut-ins" are means of grace ofttimes to whole communities.

It is known to many that there is a most helpful system of communication established among invalids over this country. Without any formal organization the following objects are aimed at: 1. To relieve the weariness of the sick-room by sending and receiving letters and other tokens of remembrance; 2. To testify of the love and presence of Christ in suffering and privation; 3. To pray for one another at set times—daily at twilight hour, and weekly on Tuesday morning at ten o'clock; 4. To stimulate faith, hope, patience and courage in fellow-sufferers by the study and presentation of Bible promises.

This simple exchanging of consolation among hundreds and thousands of "shut-ins" throughout the country is in itself a ministry whose helpfulness never can be estimated. Whatever tender comfort one finds is passed to others that they may share it. Strong friendships are formed between those who have never met. The hearts of all the great scattered company are drawn into loving sympathy as they think of and pray for one another.

Those who are happy and strong, rejoicing in

health and in physical freedom, should never forget these "shut-ins." There are one or more of them in every community. There are many ways in which strength and comfort may be sent to them. A kindly letter now and then, full of cheer and **affection,** may be like an angel's visit to a weary sufferer. Or the thoughtfulness may be shown by **sending** a book or some flowers or a little basket of fruit or other token of love. In some **cases** personal visits are also practicable. There is some way, at least, in which every one may do a little to lighten **the** burden of invalidism **in some weary** sufferer; and surely **of all** such Jesus will say, "**Ye did it** unto me."

XXI.

HELPFUL PEOPLE.

> "May I reach
> That purest heaven, be to other souls
> The cup of strength in some great agony,
> Enkindle generous ardor, feed pure love,
> Be the sweet presence of a good diffused,
> And in diffusion ever more intense!"
>
> GEORGE ELIOT.

USEFULNESS is the true measure of living. Our Lord made fruit the test of discipleship. What is fruit? Is it not something which the tree bears to feed men's hunger? In discipleship, then, fruit is something that grows upon our lives which others may take and feed upon. It is anything in us or that we do which does good to others. A fruitful Christian life is one, therefore, which is a blessing to men—one that is useful and helpful.

No one cares for a tree to be covered with fruit merely to make a fine appearance; the object of fruitfulness is to feed hunger, to satisfy men's cravings. Our Lord does not ask us to have lives full of fruit merely **to** be looked at, merely to realize a certain standard of spiritual completeness. He does not want marble statues, however perfect in their cold whiteness. Moral excellence is **not** character merely, however faultless it may be. The stern old Puritan was right when, finding the silver images standing in dusty niches and learning that they were the twelve apostles, he directed **that** they should be taken down and coined and sent out **to do good.** Charles Kingsley said, " We become **like God only** as we become **of** use."

Fruit, therefore, is usefulness. We are fruitful when our lives **in some way feed** others, when **we** are personally helpful. **It** may **be** by our words; the ministry of **good** words is **very** wonderful. He who writes a book full of living, helpful thoughts which goes into the hands of the young or of the hungry-hearted, carrying inspiration, cheer, comfort or light, does a service whose value never can **be** estimated. He who uses his gift of common speech, **as** he may use it, to utter brave, helpful, encouraging, stimulating words wherever he goes, is an immeasurable blessing in the world. **He who** writes timely letters to people who need sympathy, consolation, commendation, **wise** counsel or thought**ful word** of any kind, puts secret strength into many a spirit, feeds as with hidden manna many a struggling soul. He who sends a few flowers to a sick-room or a little fruit to a convalescent friend, or calls at the door to ask after a neighbor who is ill, or remembers the poor in some practical way, or is kind to a bereft one, is scattering benedictions whose far-reaching influence for good no eye can trace. These are chiefly little ways of helpfulness, and are suggested because they are such as are possible to nearly every one.

"It is not mine to run with eager feet
  Along life's crowded way my Lord to meet;
It is not mine to pour the oil and wine,
  Or bring the purple robe or linen fine;
It is not mine to break at his dear feet
  The alabaster box of ointment sweet;
It is not mine to bear his heavy cross,
  Or suffer for his sake all pain and loss;
It is not mine to walk through valleys dim
  Or climb far mountain-heights alone with him;
He hath no need of me in grand affairs
  Where fields are lost or crowns won unawares.
Yet, Master, if I may make one pale flower
  Bloom brighter for thy sake through one short hour,
If I in harvest-fields where stray ones reap
  May bind one golden sheaf for love to keep,
May speak one quiet word when all is still,
  Helping some fainting heart to bear thy will,
Or sing one high, clear song on which may soar
Some glad soul heavenward,—I ask no more."

Not only are these little helpfulnesses possible to all, but they are the things that people need. Now and then a large thing must be done for another—men have sacrificed all in trying to help others—but, while at rare times very costly services are required, ordinarily it is the little kindnesses that are needed and that do the greatest good.

Then the ministry of helpfulness, as a rule, is one that the poor can render as well as the rich. **People** do **not** very often need money; at least a thousand times oftener they **need love** more than **money.** It is usually much better to put a new hope into a discouraged **man's** heart than to **put a** coin into his pocket. Money is good alms in its way, but, compared with the divine gifts **of** hope, courage, sympathy and affection, it is paltry and poor. Ofttimes money-aid hinders more than it helps. **It** may make **life a** little easier for a day, **but** it is almost sure **to** make the recipient less manly and noble, less courageous and independent. The best way to help people is not to lighten the burden for them, but to put new strength into their hearts that they may be able to carry their own **loads.** That is the divine way. We are told to **cast** our burden upon **the Lord,** but the promise is **not** that the Lord will carry the burden for us, but that he will strengthen our hearts that we may be able to bear our own burden.

The aim of the divine helpfulness is not to make things easy for us, but to make something of us. We need to keep this divine principle in mind in our helping of others. It is usually easier to give relief than it is to help another to grow strong. Yet in many cases relief is the poorest help we can give; the very best is inner help—that which makes one stronger, purer, truer, braver, that which makes one able to overcome. Some one has said, "To help another is the divinest privilege one can have. There are many who help us in mechanical things; there are a few who help us in our outside duties; there are perhaps only two or three who can help us in our most sacred sphere of inner life." Yet it is the latter kind of help that is most valuable. The help that in a lifetime counts for most in real blessing is an uninterrupted flow of little ministries of word, of act, of quiet influence—kindness done to every one according to the need of each at the moment. To live fifty years of such life, though not one conspicuous thing is wrought in all that time, leaves an aggregate amount of good done vastly greater than fifty years of selfish living with one great and notable public benevolence reared like a monument of stone at the close of a man's days.

Of helpful people the true Christian home presents the best illustrations. There each one lives for the others, not merely to minister in material ways **and** in services of affection, but to promote the growth of character into whatsoever things are pure, **whatsoever** things are lovely. A true husband lives to be helpful in all ways to his wife, to make her happy, to brighten **the path for her feet,** to stimulate her spiritual life and to foster and encourage in her every noble aspiration. A true wife is a helpmate **to** her husband, blessing him **with** her love and doing him good, and not evil, all **the** days of her life. Parents live for their children. **In** all this world there is no nearer approach to the divine helpfulness than is found in true parental love. The Jewish rabbins said, "God could not be everywhere, and therefore he made **mothers."**

Brothers and sisters, also, where they realize the Christian ideal of their relation to each other, are mutually helpful in all **ways.** True **brothers** shield their sisters, protecting them from harm; they encourage them in their education and **in all** their culture of mind and heart. True sisters, in turn, are their brothers' guardian angels; many a young man owes to a sweet **and gentle sister a debt** he can never repay. Especially to older sisters **are** the brothers in countless homes indebted. Many a man honored **in the world and** occupying **a place** of influence **and** power owes all that he **is to** a sister perhaps too much forgotten **or overlooked by** him, worn and wrinkled **now,** her beauty faded, living lonely and solitary, unwedded, who in the days of his youth **was a** guardian angel to him. She freely poured out for him then **the best and** richest **of her** life, giving the very blood **of her veins that he** might have more life and **richer, denying** herself even needed comforts that he, her heart's pride, might have books and might be educated and fitted for noble and successful life. **Such** brothers can never honor enough the sisters who have made such sacrifices for them.

There is a class of women in every community whom society flippantly and profanely denominates "old maids." The world ought to be told what uncrowned queens many of these women are, what undecorated heroines, what blessings to humanity, what builders of **homes,** what servants **of** others and of **Christ. In** thousands **of** instances they voluntarily remain unmarried for the sake of their families. Many of them have refused brilliant offers of marriage that they might stay at **home to** toil for younger brothers or sisters, or that they **might be** the shelter and **comfort of parents in the feebleness** of **their** advancing years. Then there are many more who have freely hidden away their own heart-hunger that they might devote themselves to good deeds for Christ **and** for humanity. A glance over the pages of history will show many a woman's name which shines in the splendor of **such** self-sacrifice. **Then in every** community and neighborhood is one whose hand has not felt the pressure of the wedding-ring because home-loved ones or the work of the Master outside seemed to need her hallowed love and her gentle service. We should learn to honor these unmarried women instead of decorating their names with unworthy epithets. Many of them are the true heroines of neighborhood or of household, the real Sisters of Charity of the communities in which they **live.** Those who sometimes speak lightly or flippantly of them, who jest and sneer at their spinsterhood, ought to uncover their heads before them in reverence and kiss the hands—wrinkled now and shriveled—which never have been clasped in marriage. One writes in true and loyal spirit of such hands, folded in **the** coffin :

"Roughened and worn with ceaseless toil and **care,**
  No perfumed grace, **no dainty** skill, had these;
  They earned for whiter hands a jeweled ease
And kept the scars unlovely for their share.
Patient and slow, they had the will to bear
  The **whole** world's burdens, but no power to seize
  The flying joys of life, the gifts that please,
The gold and gems that others find so fair.
  Dear hands where bridal-jewel **never shone,**
Whereon no lover's **kiss was ever pressed,**
Crossed in unwonted **quiet** on the breast,
  I see through tears your glory newly won,
  The golden **circlet of life's** work well done
Set with the shining **pearl of** perfect rest."

No ambition could be higher than that which seeks to be worthy of a ministry of personal helpfulness. Every disclosure of heavenly existence that has been made to us in this world shows a life devoted to unselfish serving of others. We have in the Scriptures many glimpses of angels, and these radiant beings are presented to us as ministering spirits sent forth to do service for the sake of those who shall inherit salvation. Their holiness manifests itself in love and pity, and their adoration of God leads them to serve in behalf of fallen men. Every disclosure of the character of God himself reveals in him the same quality. His name is Love, and love is not love which does not serve. Jesus was God manifest in the flesh, and he said of his own mission that he came, "not to be ministered unto, but to minister." Thus it is in serving and in helping others that we become likest angels and likest God himself. No one has begun to live who has not begun to live for others. Life is never so rich and so beautiful as when it is giving itself out the most lavishly in act and sacrifice of love. No one living in pampered self-indulgence, though wearing a jeweled crown, is half so royal in God's sight as the lowly one, obscure and untitled among men, who is living to serve.

> "Pour out thy love like the rush of a river
>   Wasting its waters, for ever and ever,
>   Through the burnt sands that reward not the giver;
>   Silent or songful, thou nearest the sea.
>   Scatter thy life as the summer shower's pouring!
>   What if no bird through the pearl-rain is soaring?
>   What if no blossom looks upward adoring?
>   Look to the life that was lavished for thee!"

There is an Oriental story of two brothers, Ahmed and Omar. Each wished to perform a deed whose memory should not fail, but which, as the years rolled on, might sound his name and praise far abroad. Omar with wedge and rope lifted a great obelisk on its base, carving its form in beautiful devices and sculpturing many a strange inscription on its sides. He left it to stand in the hot desert and cope with its gales—his monument. But Ahmed, with deeper wisdom and truer though sadder heart, digged a well to cheer the sandy waste, and planted about it tall date-palms to make cool shade for the thirsty pilgrim and to shake down fruits for his hunger.

These two deeds illustrate two ways in either of which we may live. We may think of self and worldly success and fame, living to gather a fortune or to make a name splendid as the tall sculptured obelisk, but as cold and useless to the world. Or we may make our life like a well in the desert, with cool shade about it, to give drink to the thirsty and shelter and refreshment to the weary and faint.

Which of these two ways of living is the more Christlike it is not hard to tell. Our Master went about doing good; his life was one of personal helpfulness wherever he went. If we have his spirit, we shall hold our lives and all our possessions not as our own, but as means with which to serve and bless our fellow-men. We shall regard ourselves as debtors to all men, owing to the meanest the love that works no ill to the neighbor, that seeks not its own, that strives to do good to all. Then we shall consider our white hands as none too fine to do the lowliest service, even for the most unworthy.

With this spirit in **us we shall not have to seek** opportunities for helpfulness. Then every word we speak, every smallest thing we do, every influence we send forth, our mere shadow, as we pass by, falling on need and sorrow, will prove sweet, blessed ministry of love and will impart strength and help. Such living is twice blessed: it blesses others; **it** enriches and gladdens one's own heart. Selfishness is a stagnant pool; loving service is a living stream that in doing good to others blesses itself as well and remains ever fresh and **pure.**

> "**How** many gentle, lovely lives,
>   **And** fragrant deeds that earth has known,
>   Were never writ in ink or stone!
> And yet their sweetness still survives."

XXII.
TIRED FEET.

"My feet are wearied and my hands are tired,
   My soul oppressed,
And I desire what I have long desired—
   Rest, only rest."

FATHER RYAN.

SOME time after the author's *Week-Day Religion* was issued, among the many kindly words received from different quarters regarding the book, there came this: "Mother, sister J. and I read a chapter a day, I usually reading aloud. It was in the spring, in house-cleaning time, and we were very weary every night. One evening J. said, 'Now for our chapter in *Week-Day Religion.*' My feet were very tired and sore, and I said, as I threw myself on the lounge, 'I wonder what Mr. Miller knows about tired feet?' My sister replied that we should see. It was the fifth chapter—'Cure for Care'—that we were to read that evening, and perhaps you will remember that the chapter closes with the stanza in which are these lines:

> 'And if through patient toil we reach the land
> Where *tired feet* with sandals loose may rest.'

Was not that rather a singular coincidence? I am sure that, coming as it did, it was a real word from God for me, and it brought me new strength in my weariness."

This pleasant testimony regarding a chance phrase in another volume has suggested to me for this book a whole chapter on "tired feet." The close of every day finds a great many persons with feet tired and sore. There are some people whose duties require them to walk all day. There are the men who patrol the city's streets, the guardians of our homes; there are the postmen who bring the letters to our doors; there are the messengers who are always hurrying to and fro on their errands; there are the pilgrims who travel on foot along the hard, dusty highways; there are those who follow the plough or perform other parts of the farmer's work. Then there are those whose duties require them to be on their feet most of the day, either standing or walking about. Salespeople in great busy stores are scarcely ever allowed to sit down; the same is true of those employed in many factories and mills. Indeed, the larger portion of all working-people, in all branches of industry, stand the greater part of the day. Thousands of women in their home-work rarely ever sit down during the long days to rest. Up stairs and down again, from kitchen to nursery, out to the market and to the store, in and out from early morning till late at night, these busy women are ever plodding in their housewifely duties.

> "Man's work's from sun to sun;
> Woman's work is never done."

No wonder, then, that there are many sore and tired feet at the ending of each day. How welcome night is to the armies of weary people who then drop their tools or their yardsticks, or their other implements of toil, and hurry homeward! How good it is to sit down and rest when the day's tasks are done! Certainly there ought to be a chapter somewhere specially for people with tired feet.

But what message of comfort is there for such? For one thing, there is the thought of duty done. It is always a comfort, when one is tired, to reflect that one has grown tired in doing one's proper work. A squandered day, a day spent in idleness, may not leave such tired feet in the evening, but neither does it give the sweet pleasure that a busy day gives even with its blistered or aching feet.

There is a great deal of useless standing or walking about that gets none of this comfort. There are young men who stand on the street-corners all day, and ofttimes far into the night, who must have weary feet when at last they turn homeward; yet they have in their hearts no such sweet compensating satisfaction as have those who have toiled all the long hours in some honest and honorable calling. Idleness brings only shame and self-contempt. Then there are certain kinds of occupation which give to weariness no sweetening comfort. A day spent in sinful work may make tired feet, but has no soothing for them in the evening's rest.

But all duty well done has its restful peace of heart when the tasks are finished and laid down. Conscience whispers, "You were faithful to-day. You did all that was given to you to do; you did not shirk nor skimp." And conscience is the whisper of God. But does God take notice of one's daily common work—ploughing, delivering letters, selling goods, cleaning house? Certainly he does. We serve him just as truly in our daily task-work as in our praying and Bible-reading. The woman who keeps the great cathedral clean, sweeping the dust from the aisles and from the pews, is serving her Lord as well, if her heart be right, as the gorgeously-robed minister who performs his sacred part in the holy worship. One of George MacDonald's poems teaches this in a very sweet way.

> "Methought that in a solemn church I stood.
>   Its marble acres, worn with knees and feet,
>   Lay spread from door to door, from street to street;
> Midway the form hung high upon the rood
> Of Him who gave his life to be our good;
>   Beyond, priests flitted, bowed, and murmured meet
>   Among the candles shining still and sweet;
> Men came and went, and worshiped as they could,
>   And still their dust a woman with her broom,
> Bowed to her work, kept sweeping to the door.
>   Then saw I, slow through all the pillared gloom,
>   Across the church a silent figure come.
> 'Daughter,' it said, 'thou sweepest well my floor.'—
> 'It is the Lord!' I cried, and saw no more."

The thought that we have done our duty for another day and have pleased God ought to be like soothing balm to our sore and tired feet at the end of the day. Our Master's commendation takes the sting out of any suffering endured in doing work for him. When we know that Christ in heaven has noticed our toil and has approved it, accepting it as holy service to himself, we are ready to toil another day.

Another comfort for tired feet is in the coming

of night, when one can rest. The day's tasks are finished, the rounds are all made, the store is closed, the horses are put away, the children are in bed, the housework is done, and the tired people can sit down. The tight shoes are taken off, loose slippers are substituted, and the evening's quiet begins. Who can tell the blessings that the night brings to earth's weary toilers? Suppose there were no night, no rest—that the heavy sandals could never be laid off, that one could never sit down, that there could be no pause in the toil; how terrible would life be! Night is a holy time, because it brings rest. The rest is all the sweeter, too, because the feet are tired and sore. Those who never have been weary do not realize the blessings which come with the night.

> "Night is the time for rest.
>   How sweet, when labors close,
>   To gather round an aching breast
>   The curtain of repose,
>   Stretch the tired limbs and lay the head
>   Down on our own delightful bed!"

Wonderful is the work of repair in life that goes on while we sleep. Men bring the great ships to dock after they have ploughed the waves or battled with the storms and are battered and strained and damaged, and there they are repaired and made ready to go again to sea. At night our jaded and exhausted bodies are dry-docked after the day's conflict and toils, and while we sleep the mysterious process of restoration and reinvigoration goes on; and when morning comes we are ready to begin a new day of toil and care. We lie down tired, feeling sometimes that we can never do another day's work; but the morning comes again, we rise renewed in body and spirit, full of enthusiasm and strong and brave for the hardest duties.

What a blessing is sleep! It charms away the weariness from the aching limbs; it brushes the clouds from the sky; it refills life's drained fountains. One rendering of the old psalm-verse is, "So he giveth to his beloved in sleep." Surely, God does give us many rich blessings in our sleep. Angels come with noiseless tread into our chambers and leave their holy gifts and steal away unheard. God himself comes and touches us with his benedictions while our eyes are closed in slumber; he shuts our ears to earth's noises and holds us apart from its strifes and turmoils while he builds up again in us all that the day had torn down; he makes us forget our griefs and cares, and sends sweet dreams to restore the brightness and the gladness to our tired spirits.

There is something very **wonderful in** the mystery of sleep and **in** the way God comes to us in **the** darkness and the silence to bless **us.** Father Ryan, late poet-priest of the **South, has** written so exquisitely upon God's work in the night **for his** children that no apology is made for the quoting here of almost the whole poem:

" Betimes I seem to see in dreams
　　What when awake I may not see.
　　　　Can night be God's more than the day?
　　　　Do stars, not suns, best light his way?
　Who **knoweth?** Blended lights and shades
　　Arch aisles down which he walks to me.

" **I** hear **him coming in the night**
　　Afar, and yet I **know not how;**
　　　　His steps make music low and sweet;
　　　　Sometimes the nails are in his feet.
　Does darkness give **God** better light
　　Than day to find a weary brow**?**

" **Does darkness** give man brighter rays
　　To find the God in sunshine lost?
　　　　Must shadows wrap the trysting-place
　　　　Where God meets hearts with gentlest grace?
　Who knoweth it? God hath his ways
　　For every soul here sorrow-tossed.

" The hours of day are like the waves
　　That fret against the shores **of sin:**
　　　　They touch the human everywhere,
　　　　The bright-divine fades in their glare,

And God's sweet voice the spirit craves
  Is heard too faintly in the din.

" When all the senses are awake,
    The mortal presses overmuch
      Upon the great immortal part,
      And God seems farther from the heart.
  Must souls, like skies when day-dawns break,
    Lose star by star at sunlight's touch?

" But when the sun kneels in the west
    And gradually sinks as great hearts sink,
      And in his sinking flings adown
      Bright blessings from his fading crown,
  The stars begin their song of rest
    And shadows make the thoughtless think.

" The human seems to fade away,
    And down the starred and shadowed skies
      The heavenly comes, as memories come
      Of home to hearts afar from home,
    And through the darkness after day
      Many a wingèd angel flies.

"And somehow, tho' the eyes see less,
    Our spirits seem to see the more;
      When we look thro' night's shadow-bars,
      The soul sees more than shining stars—
  Yea, sees the very loveliness
    That rests upon the golden shore."

Another comfort for tired feet is in the thought that Jesus understands the weariness. We know that his feet were tired at the end of many a day. Once we are expressly told that, being wearied with his long journey, he sat down on a well-curb to rest. He had come far through the dust and the noontide heat, and his feet were sore. All his days were busy days, for he was ever going about on errands of love. Many a day he had scarcely time to eat. Though never weary of, he was ofttimes weary in, his Father's business.

When our feet are tired after the day's tasks and journeys, it ought to be a very precious comfort to remember that our blessed Master had like experience, and therefore is able to sympathize with us. It is one of the chief sadnesses of many lives that people do not understand them, do not sympathize with them. They move about us, our neighbors and companions—even our closest friends—and laugh and jest and are happy and light-hearted, while we, close beside them, are suffering. They are not aware of our pain; and if they were, they could not give us real sympathy, because they have never had any experience of their own that would interpret to them our experience. Only those who have suffered in some way can truly sympathize with those who suffer. One who is physically strong and has never felt the pain of weariness cannot understand the weakness of another whom the least exertion tires. The man of athletic frame who can walk all day without fatigue has small sympathy with the man of feeble health who is exhausted in a mile.

When we think of the glory of Christ, it would seem to us at first that he cannot care for our little ills and sufferings; but when we remember that he lived on earth and knows our common life by personal experience, and that he is "touched with the feeling of our infirmities," we know that he understands us and sympathizes with us in every pain. When we think of him sitting weary on the well-curb after his long, hard journey, we are sure that even in heaven he knows what tired feet mean to us after our day of toil. The comfort even of human sympathy, without any real relief, puts new strength and courage into the heart of one who suffers; the assurance of the sympathy of Christ ought to lift the weary one above all weakness, above all faintness, into victorious joy.

We should remember, too, that Christ's sacred feet were wounded that our feet may be soothed in their pain and weariness and at last may stand on the golden streets of heaven. There is a legend of Christ which tells of his walking by the sea, beautiful in form, wearing brown sandals upon his feet. A poet puts it thus:

> "He walked beside the sea; he took his sandals off
> To bathe his weary feet in the pure cool wave—
> For he had walked across the desert sands
> All day long—and as he bathed his feet
> He murmured to himself, 'Three years! Three years!
> And then, poor feet, the cruel nails will come
> And make you bleed, but that blood will lave
> All weary feet on all their thorny ways.'"

There is still another comfort for tired feet in the hope of the rest that is waiting. This incessant toil is not to go on for ever. We are going to a land where the longest journeys will produce no weariness, where "tired feet with sandals loose may rest" from all that tires. The hope of heaven, shining in glory such a little way before, ought to give us courage and strength to endure whatever of pain, conflict and suffering may come to us in these short days.

> "The burden of my days is hard to bear,
> But God knows best;
> And I have prayed—but vain has been my prayer—
> For rest, sweet rest."

> "'Twill soon be o'er;
> Far down the west
> Life's sun is setting, and I see the shore
> Where I shall rest."

XXIII.

HANDS: A STUDY.

"Take my hands, and let them move
At the impulse of Thy love."
F. R. HAVERGAL.

"The folded hands seem idle:
If folded at his word,
'Tis a holy service, trust me,
In obedience to the Lord."
ANNA SHIPTON.

MAN is the only animal that has hands; the hand, therefore, is one of the marks of man's rank and of his power. With his hand he conquers nature; with his hand he does the great works that distinguish him in God's creation; with his hand he cultivates the soil, fells the trees of the forest, tunnels the mountains, builds cities, constructs machines, belts the globe with iron rails, navigates the sea and turns all the wheels of business. It is man's hand, too, which gives form and reality to the dreams and the visions of man's brain and soul. With his hand the thinker puts his thoughts into written words, to become powers in the world; with his hand the poet weaves into graceful lines the gentle inspirations of his Muse; with his hand the musician interprets on his instrument the marvelous harmonies that move and stir men's hearts to their depths; with his hand the artist puts on his canvas the wonderful creations of his genius which immortalize his name and become part of the world's heritage of beauty.

Thus we have hints of the importance of our hands. Just what to do with them is a vital question in education. In them there are great possibilities of power and of usefulness. A distinguished author, when he saw the marble image of an infant's hand, wrote of it something like this: that it ought to be kept until the child had grown to womanhood and then to old age; until the hand had felt the pressure of affection and returned it; until it had worn the wedding-ring; until it had nursed babies and buried them; until it had gathered the flowers of earth's pleasure and been pierced by the thorns; until it had wrought its part in the world's work; until it had grown old, wrinkled and faded and been folded on the bosom in the repose of death; that then another cast of it in marble ought to be made, when the two hands would tell the whole story of a life.

It is intensely interesting to look at an infant's hand and to try to read its prophecy. Perhaps sleeping in the little fingers there is music which some day may thrill men's souls, or it may be that hidden away in them there are pictures which by and by will be made to live on the canvas, or possibly there are poems whose magic lines will some time breathe inspirations for many lives; at least, there must be folded up in the baby's chubby fingers countless beautiful things which will take form through the years as the hands do their allotted task-work. It is interesting to look at the little hand and to wonder what it will do.

Then it is interesting, when a hand is folded in the coffin, to look at it and to think of all it has done—its victories, its achievements, its beneficences; or perchance of the evil it has wrought—the hurt it has given to human lives, the suffering it has caused, the seeds of sin it has scattered. The story of all this the cold, still hand tells.

Our hands should be trained to do their best; all the possibilities in them should be developed. No doubt God has put into many fingers music which has never been drawn out, and pictures which have never been painted upon canvas, and beauty which has never charmed men's eyes, and noble beneficences which have never been wrought in acts. We should seek to bring out all that God has hidden in our hands. The things they were made to do we should strive to teach them to do. We should train them, also, to perform all their work carefully and thoroughly—always to do their best. Even the smallest things, that seem insignificant, we should do as well as we can. That is the way God works. The most minute animalculæ—millions of which swim in a drop of water—are as perfect in all their functions as are the largest of God's creatures. We do not know what is small or what is great in this world. Little things may be seeds of future great things; from the most infinitesimal acts stupendous results may come.

> "From things we call little Thine eyes
> See great things looking out."

Our hands, therefore, should be trained to do always their best work. It is a shame to do anything in a slovenly way. It is a shame to work negligently, to slight what we are set to do, to hurry through our tasks, marring the workmanship we ought to fashion just as carefully if it be but the writing of a postal-card or the dusting of a room or the building of a coal-shed as if it were the painting of a great picture, the furnishing of a palace or the erection of a cathedral.

Our hands should be ready always for duty. For a time the child does not find anything for its hands to do but to play; soon, however, it begins to discover tasks, for life is duty. Youth is full of bright dreams. Its earlier outlook paints life as pleasure only, but soon the aspect changes, the glamour fades out, and something harder and sterner emerges as duty begins to press its claims. Life's responsibility, when realized, is very serious and starts grave thoughts. It may be a burden to lift, a duty to do, a cross to bear; yet to decline it is to fail.

> "Life is a burden: bear it;
> Life is a duty: do it;
> Life is a thorn-crown: wear it.
> Though it break your heart in twain,
> Though the burden crush you down,
> Close your lips and hide your pain:
> First the cross, and then the crown."

Our hands should be loyal. They should never be withheld from duty. The question of pain or cost we should never raise. Sometimes we may have to grasp thorns, and the thorns will pierce our hands and leave them bleeding, yet we should not shrink even then from loyalty to duty. We can never forget how the hands of Christ were pierced and mangled in making redemption for us. They were beautiful hands; they were soft and gentle—so gentle that they would not break a bruised reed; they were healing hands and hands that were ever scattering blessings; yet the cruel nails tore them. He might have turned away from his cross, but he never faltered. With white face and steady step he went straight on to death. Thus the most beautiful hands in all the universe to-day are wounded hands.

Indeed, the wounds are the very marks of glory on the hands of Christ. There is a strange legend of old Saint Martin. He sat one day in his monastery cell busily engaged in his sacred studies, when there was a knock at his door. "Enter!" said the monk. The door swung open, and there appeared a stranger of lordly look, in princely attire. "Who art thou?" asked Saint Martin.—"I am Jesus Christ," was the answer. The confident bearing and the commanding tone of the visitor would have awed a man less wise than Saint Martin, but he simply gave his visitor one deep, searching, penetrating glance, and then quietly asked, "Where is the print of the nails?" The monk had seen that this one indubitable mark of Christ's person was wanting. There were no nail-scars on those jeweled hands, and the kingly mien and the brilliant dress of the pretender were not enough to prove his claim while the print of the nails was wanting. Confused by the monk's searching question and his base deception exposed, the prince of evil—so the legend runs—quickly fled away from the sacred cell. The hands of our Saviour are known by the print of the nails. In heaven we shall know him by his wounded hands. The most beautiful hands may not then be the softest, the smoothest, but may be hardened with toil or torn in struggle.

We may go through life and keep our hands very white, unroughened, unwounded, yet at the end we may find that they have wrought nothing, won nothing. When an army comes home from victorious war, it is not the regiment with the full ranks of unscarred men that the people cheer most loudly, but the regiment with only a remnant of soldiers, and these bearing the marks of many a battle. Hands scarred from conflict with life's enemies are more beautiful when held up before God than hands white and unwounded and covered with flashing jewels, because the scars tell of toil and battle.

Many a good man seems to live in vain in this world. He toils hard, but gathers nothing; he seems unsuccessful all his days; the things he undertakes do not prosper. He is a good man, faithful, conscientious, prayerful, honest and diligent, yet he appears to have no earthly reward. His life is one long discouragement, one unbroken struggle with unfavorable circumstances and conditions. The burden of care never lightens and the shadow of disappointment never lifts. He dies a poor man with hands rough and scarred and empty. His neighbor, close beside him, seems to have only success, and never failure. No disappointment comes to him; everything he touches prospers. Without toil or struggle or wounding, his hands are filled with earth's treasures. But when God looks upon the two men's hands, it may be that he will honor most the empty hands with the knotted joints and the marks of toil and struggle and suffering.

> "There were two princes doomed to death;
> Each loved his beauty and his breath;
> 'Leave us our life, and we will bring
> Fair gifts unto our lord the king.'

> "They went together. In the dew
> A charmèd bird before them flew.

Through sun and thorn one followed it:
Upon the other's arm **it lit.**

"A rose whose faintest flush was worth
All buds that ever blew on earth
One climbed the rocks to reach. **Ah, well!**
Into the other's breast it **fell.**

"Weird jewels such as fairies wear,
When moons go out, to light their hair,
One tried to touch on ghostly **ground:**
Gems of **quick fire the other found.**

"One with the dragon fought to **gain**
The enchanted fruit, and fought **in vain;**
The other breathed the garden's air,
And gathered precious apples there.

"Backward to the imperial gate
One took his fortune, one his fate.
One showed sweet gifts from sweetest lands;
The other, **torn** and empty hands.

"At bird and rose and gem and fruit
The king was sad, the king was **mute;**
At last he slowly said, 'My son,
True treasure is not lightly won.

"'Your brother's hands, wherein you see
Only these scars, show more to me
Than if a kingdom's price I found
In place of each forgotten wound.'"

Our hands should be trained to gentle ministries. **It** would be pleasant **to think of** what a hand— just a **common** hand without money or gifts of any kind—can do to bless, to inspire, to comfort, to soothe, to help. A dying father lays his hand upon the head of his child in parting benediction, and through all his life the child feels the touch and is blessed by its memory. A baby wakes in the darkness and cries out in terror; the mother reaches out her hand and lays it upon her little one, and it is instantly quieted. You are sick and hot with fever and a friend comes in and lays a soft, cool hand upon your burning brow, and a delicious sense of soothing thrills you. You are in sore affliction, sitting with breaking heart in your home, out of which the light has gone; there seems no comfort for you. Then one comes in and sits down beside you; he scarcely speaks, but he takes your hand in his and holds it with warm, gentle pressure. It may be a rough, hard hand or a large, awkward hand, but there flows through it to your soul a current of loving sympathy and of strengthful inspiration which seems to fill up your heart's drained fountains. The friend goes away without having spoken a dozen words, but you are conscious of a wonderful uplifting. You go out some morning discouraged and heavy-hearted; you do not see the blue sky overhead, for your eyes are downcast on the dull earth, where only clods and cobbles can be seen. Something has cast a shadow over you. Suddenly in the way a friend meets you and accosts you in cheerful tone; reaching out his hand, he grasps yours with great heartiness and holds it for a moment tight in his own warm clasp while he looks into your face and speaks an earnest, whole-souled greeting. He goes his way and you hurry on in yours, but now you look up and see that there is blue sky over your head; the shadow has lifted and the sunshine has entered your soul. Your friend's handshake did it all.

At the Beautiful gate lay a lame man reaching out his hand for alms. Two men approached, and the beggar craved a money-gift. The men had no money to give, but in the name of Christ they bade him rise up and walk; then one of them gave him his hand to help him to his feet. We say the age of miracles is past, but yet everywhere consecrated human hands are helping fallen ones to rise. Thousands who are in heaven to-day were saved through the ministry of a human hand that at the right moment was reached out in sympathy or in helpfulness to enable them to rise.

These are hints only of the possibilities of blessing which God has hidden away in our hands. Even without money and without words we may perform a wonderful ministry of good simply with our hands. The power that is in their touch or in their clasp is almost infinite. There is a possible ministry of incalculable influence in our ordinary handshaking. Every day as we pass along come unnumbered opportunities to do great good simply by the reaching out of our hands to those who are tempted or discouraged or sorrowing, or who have fainted and fallen in the strife. We ought to give our hands to Christ in consecration; we ought to let our heart flow out through our hands that with every hand-grasp and every touch our best love may go forth to those who need its healing, inspiring ministry. God wishes our hands to be always ready to minister to those who are in need. No other work in this world is so important as this. No matter what we are doing, when the call of human distress reaches our ear we must drop everything and be quick to respond. Mrs. Browning has put this truth in very striking phrase in a passage in "Aurora Leigh." In a company of working-girls one of them flippantly announces that another, who is absent, is dying, and then chatters on about the poor sick girl as if she were a block of wood. But there is one in the party whose heart is moved.

"Marian rose up straight,
And, breaking through the talk and through the work,
Went outward, in the face of their surprise,
To Lucy's home to nurse her back to life
Or down to death. She knew by such an act
All place and grace were forfeit in the house,
Whose mistress would supply the missing hand
With necessary, not inhuman, haste,
And take the blame. But pity, too, had dues:
She could not leave a solitary soul
To founder in the dark while she sat still
And lavished stitches on a lady's hem,
As if no other work were paramount.
'Why, God,' thought Marian, 'has a missing hand
This moment Lucy wants a drink, perhaps.
Let others miss me; never miss me, God.'"

The old legend says that once three young ladies disputed about their hands, as to whose were the most beautiful. One of them dipped her hand in the pure stream, another plucked berries till her fingers were pink, and the third gathered flowers whose fragrance clung to her hands. An old haggard woman passed by and asked for some gift, but all refused her. Another young woman, plain and with no claim to beauty of hand, satisfied her need. The old woman then said, "It is not the hand that is washed in the brook, nor the hand tinted with red, nor the hand garlanded and perfumed with flowers, that is most beautiful, but the hand that gives to the poor." As she spoke her wrinkles were gone, her staff was thrown away, and she stood there an angel from heaven.

This is only a legend, but its judgment is true: the beautiful hands are those that minister in Christ's name to others.

Sometimes the hands can only be folded in quietness, unable longer to toil or do battle or perform active service of good. But even folded hands need not be useless. It is a sad pity when hands that are strong and full of life and power are folded in indolence or cowardice.

> "Some hands fold where other hands
> Are lifted bravely in the strife,
> And so through ages and through lands
> Move on the two extremes of life."

But when through physical illness or through maiming on the field our hands can no more labor or bear the sword or do their gentle deeds, we should not repine. God never asks impossibilities, and he is pleased with sweet resignation when in his providence we can no longer take our place amid his active workers. The most acceptable service we can then render to him is a ministry of joy and praise while we submit to his loving will and are quiet under his afflicting hand. But even folded hands may still be hands of blessing: they may be reached up to God in prayer and intercession, and may draw down upon other lives rich benedictions.

At last the busiest hands must lie folded on the bosom in the stillness of death, but the things we have done in this world shall not perish when the hands that wrought them are mouldering to dust. Touches of beauty which we have left on other lives shall never fade out; the thrill of new strength given by our warm hand-clasp shall go on for ever in quickened life; the fallen one lifted up by us and saved shall walk eternally in glory. The seeds our hand has scattered shall grow into plants of immortal beauty. When we rest from our labors, the work of our hands shall follow us. Men journey now thousands of miles to look upon the paintings of artists whose hands for centuries have wrought no beauty; ages and ages hence, in heaven, angels and redeemed men shall look with rapturous joy upon some touch of beauty put yesterday in a human soul by a lowly consecrated hand of earth.

XXIV.

LEARNING OUR LESSONS.

> "I often think I cannot spell
>   The lesson I must learn,
> And then in weariness and doubt
>   I pray the page **may** turn;
>
> "**But** time goes on, and soon I find
>   I was learning all the while,
> And words which seemed most dimly **traced**
>   Shine out with rainbow smile."
>
>   FRANCES RIDLEY **HAVERGAL**.

WE are all scholars at school. **In our** present life we never get out of our class-forms; **our** real living lies on beyond, and here all is education. We are at school not merely when we are bending over our Bibles, listening to sermons, reading good books or sitting at the feet of our teachers, but also when we are at our tasks, when we are in the midst of life's busy scenes and when we are passing through experiences **of** difficulty and trial.

We have our school-books from **which to learn** our lessons; among these the Bible is **first**. It is a wonderful book. **God** is its author; its **lessons are** patterned from the heavenly life, which is the standard in all our earthly training; it contains all that we need to learn; its lessons, fully mastered, will bring us to heaven's gates.

There are also secondary text-books in which Bible-lessons are set for us in different forms. In the lives of good people about us we have these lessons—not written out with ink on white paper, but transcribed in indelible letters on mystic life-pages. We see there the lessons not in words merely, as commands for obedience, as rules for action or as heavenly patterns for earthly attainment, but brought down out of the skies and wrought into actual life.

In providence, too, we have another secondary text-book; in this God gives us special lessons. Here, ofttimes, he compels us to learn the things we do not want to learn. Here the school is disciplinary; our Father so deals with us as to subdue our willfulness, to check our waywardness, to quell our rebelliousness, to correct our ideas of life and to cleanse our hearts of the poison of sin that lurks in them. Many times this part of our school-experience is painful, but its results are full of blessing.

"The darkness in the pathway of man's life
Is but the shadow of God's providence

> By the great Sun of wisdom cast thereon,
> And what is dark below is light in heaven."

In life itself we have a "practice-school;" the things we learn from our text-books we there try to get into our life. For example, our morning lesson is the duty of patience. We understand quite clearly, as we bend over the Bible-page, what the lesson means and what it requires us to do. Then with prayer for grace we shut the book and go out into the world to take up our tasks and to meet the experiences of the day. On all sides people's lives touch ours—not always sympathetically, sometimes in such a way as would naturally disturb us, arouse antagonism in us, provoke us to anger, or at least ruffle our calm. Now comes in our morning lesson on patience. The learning of it in mere words was a simple enough matter, but probably we shall find that it is not so simple a matter to practice it. It is much easier to get a text of Scripture fastened in our memory than to get the lesson of the text wrought into our life. Nevertheless, there the lesson stands, confronting our eyes all the day.

> " Be patient, patient, and the hasty word
> Which loose will raven like the evening wolf
> Hold in the bars of safety. Bear the cross

> Fibre of things, the thousand vexing cares,
> With such a sweet, ennobling fortitude,
> Such gentle bravery, that the heart will find
> In the still fold a fairer victory
> Than in the stormy field, and home itself
> Win to rejoicing peace."

Part of our day's task is to apply this lesson, allowing it to hold in check all the impulses toward impatience which the passing experiences may stir within us. Our morning text is set to stand monitor over our dispositions, words and conduct, and its mission is to bring all our life to its lofty standard.

Or the lesson may be, "Love . . . seeketh not her own." We look at it first merely as a rule, a principle, apart from its relation to our own life, and we give it our most hearty approval; it is Christlike, we say, to live so. Again, we go out amid the strifes, the ambitions, the clashings and the competitions of life, and begin our day. We have learned our lesson; now we are to practice it. This we soon find is very hard. It is against nature; there is a law in our members which at once begins to war against the new idea of love which as disciples of Christ we have taken into our heart. To obey our morning lesson requires the putting of self under our feet, and self violently resists such humiliation. Still, there the lesson stands in shining letters, and it is our duty, as obedient and diligent scholars, to learn it—that is, to strive to get it wrought into our own life.

The same is true whatever the lesson may be. It is one thing to learn well what the lessons are and quite another thing to learn to live them. Most of us acquire life's lessons very slowly. Some of us are dull scholars; some of us are careless, loving play better than school, not taking life seriously, not diligently applying ourselves to our lessons; some of us are willful and obstinate, indisposed to submit to our teachers and to the rules of the school. Thus many of us come to the close of our school-days without having learned much—certainly without having attained a large measure of that culture of character and that discipline of life which it is the end of all spiritual training to produce. We are not obedient to our heavenly visions. We know, but we do not. We learn our lessons, but fail ofttimes to live them.

All life-lessons are slowly learned. It is the work of years to school our wayward wills into uncomplaining submissiveness, our hard, proud, selfish hearts into soft, gentle thoughts, and our harsh, chattering tongues into sweet, quiet speech.

The natural process of spiritual growth is first the blade, then the ear, then the full corn in the ear, and these developments require time. We cannot have blade, ear and full corn—bud, blossom and ripened fruit—all in one day. We must be content to learn slowly the great lessons of life. Ofttimes, too, we have to take the same lesson over and over again. In one of Miss Havergal's suggestive poems she illustrates this by the experience of a pupil who thought she knew her lesson well, but the teacher came and gravely though lovingly shook her head, and returned the book with the mark in the same place: the pupil was to take the same lesson again. This time it was mastered every word. We commend the faithfulness and the wisdom of the teacher who will allow no pupil to pass any lesson that is not mastered. It is far truer kindness, also, to the pupil to insist that he shall take his lesson over again, rather than allow it to pass and to remain a leaf dropped out, a lesson not learned. So, when we do not have our lessons learned, God gives them to us again.

> "Is it not often so—
>   That we only learn in part,
> And the Master's testing-time may show
>   That it was not quite 'by heart'?

> Then he gives, in his wise and patient grace,
>   That lesson again,
> With the mark still set in the selfsame place.
>
> "Then let our hearts 'be still'
>   Though our task is turned to-day;
> Oh, let him teach us what he will
>   In his own gracious way,
> Till, sitting only at Jesus' feet,
>   As we learn each line,
> The hardest is found all clear and sweet."

When we look at one who seems to have acquired all life's lessons, it is a great comfort to us who are so far behind him to know that he began low down in the Master's school and learned his lessons in just the same slow, painful way in which we have to learn them. Thus Saint Paul, referring to himself, said, "I have learned, in whatsoever state I am, therein to be content." The statement is remarkable because such contentment is so rare even among Christian people. But there is one word in this bright record of spiritual attainment which has immeasurable comfort for us common mortals in our struggles after the same spirit. Saint Paul says that he had *learned* to be content. We know, then, that he was not always thus; at the first he probably chafed amid discomforts and had to learn his lesson as we have to learn ours.

Contentment did not come naturally to him any more than it does to ordinary Christians; it was not a special apostolic gift which came with his divine appointment to his sacred ministry. He *learned* to be contented. Probably it was no easy attainment for him, and was reached only through many a struggle and through long and painful self-discipline.

Such a glimpse into the inner history of a saintly life ought to have its encouragement for us. Life's great lessons cannot be learned by any one without persistent and patient effort, but they can be mastered by any one who is in Christ's school and who will be earnest, diligent and faithful. The paths that others have trodden before us to honor and nobleness are open also to our feet.

But the question comes up from a vast multitude of men and women who are dissatisfied with their attainments and long to grow better, "How can we get these beautiful lessons wrought into life?" We know very well that we ought to be patient, sweet-tempered, unselfish, thoughtful and contented; but when we begin to reach after these qualities, we find them far away and unattainable. The bright stars in the sky seem scarcely farther beyond our reach, when we stand on one of earth's lofty peaks, than do the spiritual lessons set for us when we strive to get them into our life. Nothing makes us more conscious of our fallen state than our attempts to realize in ourselves the beauty of Christ. We soon discover that moral perfection is inaccessible to any human climbing. We are like birds with broken wings—made to fly into the heart of the sky, but unable to do more than flutter along low down and close to the earth. So the question recurs perpetually, "How can we ever master these lessons that are set for us? They are hard enough for angels; how, then, can fallen mortals ever learn them?"

At last we are compelled to confess that we can never learn them save in Christ's school. He says, "Learn of me and ye shall find rest unto your souls." There is a little prayer—said to have been Fénelon's prayer—which recognizes and voices this helplessness of humanity in a most striking way. It is in these words: "Lord, take my heart, for I cannot give it; and when thou hast it, oh keep it, for I cannot keep it for thee; and save me in spite of myself, for Jesus Christ's sake." Each clause of the short prayer fits our hearts.

"Lord, take my heart, for I cannot give it." We want to give our heart to Christ, but we are conscious of something holding us down, so that we cannot press ourselves into Christ's hands. An old writer says, "Of what avail are wings, when we are fast bound by iron chains?" That is our picture—like an eagle, eager to fly away into the sky, but chained to a rock. Unless Christ take us and lift us away, breaking our chains, we never can fly into his bosom.

"And when thou hast it, oh keep it, for I cannot keep it for thee." Again it is the plaint of every heart that the prayer voices. Our life may be laid sweetly in Christ's bosom to-day, but unless he shall keep it, folding about it his own mighty arms, it will fall out again into darkness. We cannot keep our heart for Christ.

"And save me in spite of myself." Pitiable as is the confession of weakness in these words, we know well that if ever we are saved it must be in spite of ourselves.

So we are brought to realize that the lessons of Christian life can be learned only when we have Christ not merely for a Teacher, but also for a Saviour; we never can be Christlike unless Christ shall lift us up by his grace. But by receiving Christ into our hearts we enter the family of God on earth and become heirs of glory. The

first thing, therefore, in learning our lessons **is to
have Christ living in us**; then our lives shall **grow**
from within into all moral loveliness.

Another secret in spiritual education is to seek at
once to live every **lesson** we are taught. There **is**
not a line of divine truth which is not intended in
some way to affect our lives. Too many **of us** are
content **to** know the lesson, and then **not** do **it**.
Divine truth is not given to us merely for informa-
tion, to make **us** intellectually intelligent. The
Bible is a book for action. It is designed to **be a
guide to us.** A guide's duty **is** not to deliver lect-
ures **to** tourists telling them of the richness **and the**
picturesqueness of the country that lies beyond **the**
hills, describing the path that leads to it, and vividly
painting the beautiful scenery along the way. A
guide's duty is to take his party along the path, leading them safely through all dangers, and conducting
them at last into the beautiful country that their
own eyes may see it. The word of God is given to
us to be our guide; that is, every sentence of it is
a call to us to move onward, away from some **sin**
or danger or self-indulgence, to some **fresh duty,**
some higher plane of living, some new holiness,
some richer experience.

Every line **of the Bible,** therefore, is a lesson set

for us which we are to learn—not intellectually alone, but by doing what the lesson teaches. We can never really learn the words of Scripture save by doing them. For example, here is a music-book—a book with notes on a musical staff, and with words also which are meant to be sung to the notes. The man who asks me to buy this book says it will teach me music. I buy the book and take it home, and sit down in my quiet library to learn my lessons. I memorize all the explanations and definitions till I can open the book at any tune and tell what the key is and what the notes are. Yet I have never opened my mouth to try to sing; I cannot even run a scale. Every one knows that music is not learned in that way. The pupil must practice the notes; he must make the sounds indicated. It is just so with the Bible. The only way to learn its lessons is to do them. Merely discovering what our duties are will not take us a step onward in Christian life. We can learn only by doing. When the path has been pointed out to us, we must set our feet in it. When the song has been written out for us, we must sing it. When the land has been described to us, we must move forward and take possession of it. When the picture has been visioned to us, we must paint it on the canvas of our soul.

When the duty has been revealed to us, we must hasten to carry our whole soul into it.

We should take, also, the lessons of experience as we learn them, and carry them forward to enrich our life. It certainly is a profitless living which gets nothing from its past. We should train ourselves to look honestly at our own past and with unsparing fidelity to note the mistakes we have made and the wrong things we have committed. Then, having discovered the errors and mistakes we have made, we should straightway formulate for ourselves the lessons which our experience is designed to teach, and instantly begin to live by the new wisdom thus acquired. Our past is of use to us only as it helps us make our future better. Its errors should be shunned, its mistakes avoided. It certainly is weak and poor living, unworthy of an immortal being, which gathers nothing from experience and goes on day after day and year after year merely repeating the old routine of negligence and failure, with no progress, learning nothing, growing no gentler, no stronger, no braver, no more Christlike. Our lives should be like opening rosebuds, every day unfolding some new beauty. The Christ in us should break through the crust of our outer life as the lamplight pours through the porcelain shade, and appear more and more in our character, in our disposition, in our words and conduct.

The celebrated statue of Minerva which stood in the Acropolis at Athens was renowned for its graceful beauty and its exquisite sculpture, but there was in it another feature which no close observer failed to notice. Deeply engraven in the buckler on the statue was the image of Phidias, the sculptor; it was so deftly impressed that it could be effaced only by destroying the work of art itself. In like manner, in the life of every true Christian is the image of Christ; it is so inwrought in the character, in the disposition, in the whole being, that it cannot be destroyed. It is toward the filling out of this likeness that all Christian culture aims. All our lessons are in growing Christlike. In any circumstances we need but to ask, "How would my Master act if he were in my place?" and then strive to do what he would do.

Thus all life is school to us. The lessons are set for us hour by hour. We think we are in this world to work, to achieve success, to accomplish something that will remain when we are gone; really, however, we are not here to work, but to be trained. Everything in our life is educational and disciplinary. Duty is but lesson-practice; work is for development more than for results; trial is for the testing **and the** strengthening **of our powers; sorrow** is for the purifying of our souls. Many times our lessons are hard and our experiences are **bitter;** but if we are patient and faithful, we shall some day see that our Teacher never set us a wrong lesson, never required of us a needless self-denial, never called us **to** pass through an unblessed discipline, never corrected us but for our **profit that** we might be partakers of his holiness.

" Some time, when all life's lessons **have** been learned,
 And sun and stars for evermore have **set,**
 The things which our weak judgments here have spurned,
  The things o'er which we grieved with lashes wet,
 Will flash before us, out of life's dark night,
  As stars shine most in deeper tints of blue,
 And we shall see how all God's plans were right,
  And how what seemed reproof **was love** most true."

XXV.

BROKEN LIVES.

"Oh, to be nothing, nothing,
　　Only to lie at his feet,
A broken and emptied vessel
　　For the Master's use made meet—
Emptied, that he might fill me
　　As forth to his service I go;
Broken, that so unhindered
　　His life through me might flow!"

THERE are few entirely unbroken lives in this world; there are few men who fulfill their own hopes and plans without thwarting or interruption at some point. Now and then there is one who in early youth marks out a course for himself and then moves straight on in it to its goal, but most persons live very differently from their own early dreaming. Many find at the close of their career that in scarcely one particular have they realized their own life-dreams; at every point God has simply set aside their plans and substituted his own.

There are some lives whose plans are so completely thwarted that their story is most pathetic as we read it; yet we have but to follow it through to the end to see that the broken life was better and more effective than if its own plan had been carried out.

The story of Harriet Newell is an illustration of a broken life. Listening to the cries of the perishing and to the call of duty, she sailed away as a missionary. She had in her heart a great purpose and a great hope. She planned to devote her rich and beautiful life, with all its powers of love, sympathy and helpfulness, to the cause of Christ in heathen lands; she hoped to be a blessing to thousands as she lived a sweet life amid the darkness and heathenism and told the story of Christ's cross to perishing ones. With these desires and hopes in her soul she sailed away to India, but she was never permitted to do any work for Christ among those she so yearned to save. Driven from inhospitable shores and drifting long at sea, first her baby died, and then she herself soon sank into death's silence. In one short year she was bride, missionary, mother and saint.

Truly, her life seemed a broken one—defeated, a failure. Not one of the glorious hopes of her own consecration was realized. She told no heathen sister of the love of Christ; she taught no little child the way of salvation; she had no opportunity to live a sweet life in the midst of the black heathenism she so wanted to bless; yet that little grain of wheat let fall into the ground and dying there has yielded a wonderful harvest. The story of her life has kindled the missionary spirit in thousands of other women's souls. Harriet Newell, dying with all her heart's holy hopes unrealized, has done far more for missions by the inspiration of her heroic example and by the story of her life's sacrifice than she could ever have done in the longest life of the best service in the field. The broken life became more to the world than it could have become by the carrying out of its own plans.

The story of David Brainerd is scarcely less pathetic. At Northampton his grave is seen beside that of the fair young girl whom he loved, but did not live to wed. His death seemed untimely, like the cutting down of a tree in the springtime when covered with buds just ready to burst into bloom and then grow into rich fruit. In that noble life, as men saw it, there were wondrous possibilities of usefulness. The young man seemed fitted to do a great work and he had consecrated himself on God's altar with large hopes of service for his Master; but all these hopes and expectations were buried in the early grave of the young missionary, and to human eyes there was nothing left but a precious memory and a few score of Indian Christians whom he had been permitted to lead to the Saviour. His seemed indeed a broken life. But we must not write our judgments on God's work until it is finished. A skillful hand inspired by tender love gathered up the memorials of the fragment of consecrated life Brainerd had lived and put them into a little biography. The book was wafted over the sea, and Henry Martyn, busy in his studies, read it. The result was that that brilliant young student felt his own heart fired with missionary zeal as he pondered the story of Brainerd's brief but beautiful life, and was led to devote himself, with all his splendid gifts, to God for India. Thus the broken life of Brainerd became the inspiration in a distant country of another noble missionary career. And who can tell what other lives through this glorious missionary century have likewise been kindled at young Brainerd's grave?

The story of Henry Martyn is that of another broken life. He went to India, and there laid his magnificent powers upon God's altar. He wrought with earnestness and with great fervor, but at the end there seemed to be small gain to the cause of Christ from all his toil and self-denial. Then, broken down, sick and dying, he turned his face homeward and dragged himself in great suffering and weakness "as far as that dreary khan at Tocat by the Black Sea, where he crouched under the piled-up saddles to cool his burning fever against the earth, and there died alone among unbelievers, no Christian hand to tend his agony, no Christian voice to speak in his ear the promises of the Master whom, as it seemed to men, he had so vainly served." Both these young missionary lives appeared to be entire failures, wasted lives, costly ointment poured out to no purpose; but from the grave of Brainerd at Northampton and from the desolate resting-place of Henry Martyn at Tocat has come much—who can tell how much?—of the inspiration of modern missions. God broke the alabaster caskets which held their rich lives that the fragrance might flow out to fill all the world.

There is another class of broken lives—of those who, disappointed in their own early hopes and turned aside, yet live to realize in other lines and spheres than those of their enthusiastic choosing far nobler things than they could ever have wrought had their own plans been carried out. John Kitto, when a lad, met with a misfortune which seemed altogether to unfit him for usefulness. By a terrible fall he received severe bodily injuries and was rendered totally and permanently deaf. The result was the turning of his life into new channels, in which he achieved a marvelous success, becoming one of the most voluminous and most instructive of all writers of books to help in the illumination and interpretation of the Bible. God suffered the breaking and the complete shattering of the boy's hopes that the man might do a far grander work in other lines. But for the misfortune that seemed to unfit him for any useful pursuit and to leave him a hopeless and pitiable object of charity, he probably would never have been more than an obscure mechanic; but now his books are in hundreds of thousands of libraries and his name is a familiar household word in nearly every intelligent Christian home in the English-speaking world.

A young man at the completion of his theological course offered himself as a missionary, and was accepted. Full of glowing earnestness and animated by a deep love for Christ, he sailed away to a foreign field, hoping there to spend his life in telling the story of redemption. After a brief experience, however, he was compelled to abandon his missionary work and with great grief and reluctance return to his native country. Not only was his health broken, but he had permanently lost his voice in the experiment, and was thus disqualified for the work of preaching anywhere. It was a sad hour to the ardent young minister when this fact became apparent to his mind. His was indeed a broken life. All his hopes and expectations of consecrated service lay like dead flowers at his feet; he seemed doomed thenceforward to an inactive and a fruitless life.

So it appeared at that moment. But, returning to his own land, he soon found work for his brain and pen in editorial lines, and entered upon a service of incalculable value to the Church. In this field for thirty busy years he wrought incessantly for his Master. God suffered his life as a missionary to be broken that in another sphere—one no less important—he might render a service probably greater far than he could have rendered had he wrought all his thirty years in a foreign land.

These are only illustrations of what God does with earth's "broken lives" that are truly consecrated to him. He even seems sometimes to break them himself that they may become more largely useful. At least, he can use broken lives in his service just as well as whole ones; indeed, it often appears as if men cannot do much **for** God and for the blessing of the world until they are "broken vessels."

God seems to be able to do little with earth's unbroken things, and therefore almost always he chooses broken things with which to **do** his work in this world. It was with broken pitchers that Gideon won his great victory; it was on broken pieces of the ship that Saint Paul and his companions escaped **to** land after their shipwreck; it was by the breaking of Mary's alabaster box that **the Master** was anointed and the world filled with the gracious perfume of love; it was by the breaking of the precious humanity of Jesus that redemption was made for man. It is by the breaking of our hearts that we become acceptable offerings on God's altar; it is by broken lives—broken by pain, trouble and sorrow—that God chiefly blesses the world; it is by the shattering of our little human plans that **God's** great perfect plan goes on in us and through **us**; it is by crushing our lives until their beauty seems entirely destroyed that God makes us blessings in this world. Not many men nor many women without suffering in some form become largely helpful to others. It seems as if **we could** not be fit instruments for God to **use to**

speak his words and breathe the songs of his love and carry to others the benedictions of his grace until his chastening hand has done its sharp, keen work upon our lives.

A piece of wood once bitterly complained because it was being cut and filled with rifts and holes; but he who held the wood and whose knife was cutting into it so remorselessly did not listen to the sore complaining. He was making a flute out of the wood he held, and was too wise to desist when entreated so to do. He said, "Oh, thou foolish piece of wood, without these rifts and holes thou wouldest be only a mere stick for ever—a bit of hard black ebony with no power to make music or to be of use in any way. These rifts that I am making in thee, which seem to be destroying thee, will change thee into a flute, and thy sweet music then shall charm the souls of men. My cutting thee is the making of thee, for then thou shalt be precious and valuable and a blessing in the world."

This little parable, suggested by a passage in an eloquent sermon, needs no explanation. The flute whose music is so sweet as we hear its notes in the great orchestra was made a flute only by the knife that filled the wood with rifts and holes which seemed its destruction. Without these merciless cuttings it could have been for ever only a piece of dull wood, dumb and musicless. It is the same with most human lives; it is only when the hand of chastening has cut into them that they begin to yield sweet music. David could never have sung his sweetest songs had he not been sorely afflicted; his afflictions made his life an instrument on which God could breathe the music of his love to charm and soothe the hearts of men. This is the story, too, of all true poetry and true music: not till the life is broken is it ready for the Master's use. At best we are but instruments, musicless save when God breathes through us.

"We are but organs mute till a master touches the keys—
  Verily, vessels of earth into which God poureth the wine;
Harps are we, silent harps that have hung in the willow trees,
  Dumb till our heartstrings swell and break with a pulse divine."

Then we cannot even be instruments fit for God's use until our hearts have been broken by penitence and our lives rent by suffering.

There ought to be great comfort in this for those who are under God's chastening hand. His design is to fit them for nobler usefulness, to make them instruments whose keys will respond to the divine touch and through whose rifts the divine Spirit can breathe strains of holy love. We ought to be better able to endure pain and suffering when we remember what God is doing with us.

Thus we see that a life is not a failure because it is broken. Broken health is naturally discouraging; but if God be in it, we need not be disheartened: he is able to make more of us with our shattered health than we could have made of ourselves with athletic robustness. Broken life-plans appear to be failures; but when God's great plan runs on in our life, without hindrance or interruption, through the fragments of our little purposes, there is no failure. We groan over our broken days when by outside interruptions we are prevented from accomplishing the tasks we had set for ourselves in the morning; but if we give our day to God at its beginning and he chooses to assign us other things to do than those we had purposed—his things instead of our own—we ought not to say in the evening that we have had a broken day. What we call interruptions are simply God's plan breaking into ours. There is no doubt that his way is better than ours. Besides, it is necessary for us all to learn our lesson of submission, and there is need for the discipline of interruption.

> "I would have gone: God bade me stay;
> **I would have** worked: God bade me rest;
> **He broke my will** from day to day;
> He read my yearnings unexpressed,
> And said them nay."

Many of God's children are found among earth's unsuccessful ones. This world has no use for broken lives; it casts them aside and hurries on, leaving them behind. Only successful men reach earth's goals and are crowned with its crowns. **But God is** the God of the unsuccessful. Christ takes earth's "bruised reeds" and deals with them **so gently that they get back** again all **their** old beauty. No life is so broken, whether **by sorrow** or by sin, that it may not through divine grace **enter** the kingdom of God and at last be presented faultless, arrayed in heavenly brightness, before the throne of glory. Heaven is filling with earth's broken lives, but there **no life will** be broken or marred; all will **be perfect** in their beauty and complete in their blessedness, bearing the image of the Redeemer.

Many of earth's noblest and most useful **lives** appear to end in the very midst of their usefulness, to be cut off while their work is unfinished—perhaps when it is scarcely begun. We easily reconcile ourselves to the dying **of an** aged Christian, because he has filled up the allotted measure of human life. We quote the Scripture words about a shock of corn coming in in its season; probably we lay a little sheaf of wheat on the coffin or cut a sheaf on the stone set up to mark the place where the weary body sleeps.

But when a young person dies we do not have the same feeling. We do not so easily reconcile ourselves to the ending of the life. We had expected our friend to live to be old, and are sorely disappointed in his early death. We do not quote the words about the corn, nor do we put the handful of wheat in the cold fingers or carve it on the stone. We seek for emblems rather which denote too early a death, cutting on the marble an unopened bud, a broken shaft or other symbol of incompleteness.

Yet when we think more deeply of the matter, should a death in bright sunny youth or in midlife be regarded as untimely? Should the life thus cut off be considered an incomplete one? Should not Christian faith lay the ripe sheaf on the coffin of the godly young man and speak of his life, if it has been noble and true, as a shock of corn coming in in its season?

If every life is a plan of God, is not the date of

its ending part of that **plan?** We would **not call** the life of Jesus incomplete, although **he died at three and** thirty. Indeed, as he drew to the end, he said to his Father, "I have finished the work which thou gavest me to do," and with his expiring breath he cried aloud in triumph, "It is finished!" It does not, therefore, require **years to** make a **life complete. One** may die young and not depart too **soon. It is** possible for a life to remain in **this** world but **for one day** or **one** hour, and yet **be complete** according to God's plan for **it.**

To our view, **it is a broken life which is taken** away **in** the midst of great usefulness. It seems **to our** limited vision that every one should live to complete the good work he has begun. **But** this **is** by no means necessary. The work is not ours, but God's; each one of us does a little part of it, and then as we fall out another comes and does his **part** just next to ours. One may sow a field and die before the reaping-time, and another gathers the sheaves. The reaping was not **part of** the sower's work. **We** may begin something, and then be called away **before** finishing it. Evidently, the finishing was not our work, but belongs to some **other's** life-plan. We **must** not say that **a man's** life is **a broken** one because he did only a little part of some great and good work; if he was faithful, he did all that was allotted to him. God has ready some other one whose mission it is to do what we supposed it was our friend's mission to do. The poet E. R. Sill has expressed this truth in lines which are well worth quoting:

> "Fret not that thy day is gone
> And the task is still undone:
> 'Twas not thine, it seems, at all;
> Near to thee it chanced to fall—
> Close enough to stir thy brain
> And to vex thy heart in vain.
>
> "Somewhere in a nook forlorn
> Yesterday a babe was born:
> He shall do thy waiting task;
> All thy questions he shall ask,
> And the answers will be given,
> Whispered lightly out of heaven.
>
> "His shall be no stumbling feet,
> Falling when they should be fleet;
> He shall hold no broken clue;
> Friends shall unto him be true;
> Men shall love him; falsehood's aim
> Shall not shatter his good name.
>
> "Day shall nerve his arm with light,
> Slumber soothe him all the night;
> Summer's peace and winter's storm
> Help him all his will perform.
> 'Tis enough of joy for thee
> His high service to foresee."

It is, then, a lesson of faith that we should learn. We ought never to be afraid of God's providences when they seem to break up our lives and crush our hopes—even to turn us away as Christ's true disciples from our chosen paths of usefulness and service. God knows what he wants to do with us, how he can best use us and where and in what lines of ministry he would have us serve, or whether he would have us only "stand and wait." When he shuts one door, it is because he has another standing open for our feet; when he thwarts our plans, it is that his own plan may go on in us and through us; when he breaks our lives to pieces, it is because they will do more for his glory and the world's good broken and shattered than whole.

XXVI.

COMING TO THE END.

> " Life, we've been long together
>   Through pleasant and through cloudy weather.
> 'Tis hard to part when friends are dear;
> Perhaps 'twill cost a sigh, a tear;
>   Then steal away, give little warning:
>   Choose thine own time;
>   Say not 'Good-night!' but in some brighter clime
>   Bid me 'Good-morning!'"
>
> MRS. BARBAULD.

WE are always coming to the end of something; nothing earthly is long-lived. Many things last but for a day; many, for only a moment. You look at the sunset-clouds, and there is a glory in them which thrills your soul; you turn to call a friend to behold the splendor with you, and it has vanished, and a new splendor—as wondrous, though altogether different—is in its place. You cross a field on an early summer morning, and every leaf and every blade of grass is covered with dewdrops, which sparkle like millions of diamonds as the first sunbeams fall on them; but a few moments later you return, and not a dewdrop is to be seen. You walk through your garden one summer morning, and note its wondrous variety of flowers in bloom, with their marvelous tints and their exquisite loveliness; to-morrow you walk again along the same paths, and there is just as great variety and as rich beauty, but all is changed. Many of yesterday's flowers are gone, and many new ones have bloomed out.

So it is in all our personal experiences. Life is a kaleidoscope; every moment the view changes. The beautiful things of one glance are missing at the next, while new things—just as lovely, though not the same—appear in their place. The joys we had yesterday we do not have to-day, though our hearts may be quite as happy now, with gladness just as pure and deep. In a sense, to most of us, life is routine, an endless repetition—the same tasks, the same duties, the same cares, day after day, year after year; yet even in this routine there is constant change. There is an interstitial life that flows through the channel of our daily experiences and that is ever new. We meet new people, we have new things, we read new books, we see new pictures, we learn new facts, while at the same time many of the familiar things are continually dropping out of our lives. The face we saw yesterday we miss to-day, and there are new faces in the throng; the songs we sang last year we do not sing this year; the books we used to read with zest we do not care for any longer; the pleasures that once delighted us have no more charm for us; the toys that meant so much to childhood and were so real have no fascination whatever for manhood and for womanhood; the happy days of youth, with their sports and games, their schools and studies, their friendships and visions, are left behind, though never forgotten, as we pass on into actual life with its harder tasks, its rougher paths, its heavier burdens, its deeper studies, its sterner realities. So we are ever coming to the end of old things and to the beginning of new things. We keep nothing long.

This is true of our friendships. Our hearts are made to love and to cling. Very early the little child begins to tie itself to other lives by the subtle cords of affection. All through life we go on gathering friends and binding them to us by ties of varying strength, sometimes slight as a gossamer-thread and as easily broken, sometimes strong as life itself—the very knitting of soul to soul. Yet our friendships are ever changing. Some of them we outgrow and leave behind us as we pass from childhood and youth to maturity; some of them have only an external attachment, and easily fall off and are scarcely missed and leave no scar. This is true of many of our associations in business, in society, in life's ordinary comminglings. We are thrown into more or less intimate relations with people, not by any attractive affinity, any drawing of heart, but by circumstances; and, while there may be pleasant congeniality, there is no real blending or weaving together, life with life; consequently, the ending of such associations produces no sore wrench or pain, no heart-pang. All through life these friends of circumstances are changing; we have the same no two successive years.

In every true life there is an inner circle of loved ones who are bound to us by ties woven out of our very heart's fibres. The closest of these are the members of our own household. The child's first friend is the child's mother; then comes the father; and then the other members of the family are taken into the sacred clasp of the opening life. By and by the young heart reaches outside and chooses other friends from the great world of common people and out of the multitude of passing associates, and binds them to itself with friendship's strongest cords. Thus all true men and true women come up to mature years clustered about by a circle of friends who are dear to them as their own life. Our debt to our life's pure and holy friendships is incalculable; they make us what we are. The mother's heart is the child's first schoolroom. The early home-influences give their tints and hues to the whole after-life; a gentle home where only kindly words are spoken and loving thoughts and dispositious are cherished fills with tender beauty the lives that go out from its shelter. All early friendships print their own stamp on the ripening character. Our souls are like the sensitive plates which the photographer puts into his camera, which catch every image whose reflection falls upon them and hold it ready to be brought out in the finished picture. Says George MacDonald:

> "I think that nothing made is lost—
> That not a moon has ever shone,
> That not a cloud my eyes hath crossed,
> But to my soul is gone;
>
> "That all the lost years garnered lie
> In this thy casket, my dim soul,
> And thou wilt, once, the key apply
> And show the shining whole."

True in general, this is especially true of the

pure friendships of our lives. None of the impressions that they make on our lives are ever lost; they sink away into our souls, and then reappear at length in our character.

But even these tender and holy friendships we cannot keep for ever; one by one they fall off or are torn out of our lives. There are many ways of losing friends. Sometimes, without explanation, without offence or a shadow of a reason of which we know, without hint or warning given, our friend suddenly withdraws from us and goes his own way, and through life we never have hint or token of the old friendship.

> "Oh, what was the hour and the day,
>   The moment, I lost you?
> I thought you were walking my way;
>   I turned to accost you,
>
> "And silence and emptiness met
>   My word half unspoken.
>   *   *   *   *   *
>
> "Oh, what was the hour and the day,
>   The moment, you left me,
> When you went on your separate way,
>   Oh, friend, and bereft me?"

Some friends are lost to us, not by any sudden rupture, but by a slow and gradual falling apart which goes on imperceptibly through long periods, tie after tie unclasping until all are loosed, when hearts once knit together in holy union find themselves hopelessly estranged. A little bird dropped a seed on a rock. The seed fell into a crevice and grew, and at length the great rock was rent asunder by the root of the tree that sprang up. So little seeds of alienation sometimes fall between two friends, and in the end produce a separation which rends their friendship and sunders them for ever.

"No sudden treason turns
The long-accustomed loyalty to hate,
But years bring weariness for sweet content;
And fondness, daily sustenance of love,
Which use should make a tribute easier paid,
First grudged, and then withheld, the heart is starved;
And, though compassion or remorseful thought
Of happy days departed bring again
The ancient tenderness in seeming flood,
Not less it ebbs and ebbs till all is bare."

No picture could be sadder than this, but the saddest thing about it is its truthfulness and the frequency of its repetition in actual life. Many a friendship is lost by this slow process of imperceptibly growing apart.

Then, friends are lost through misunderstandings which in many cases a few honest words at first might have removed. The Scriptures say, "A whisperer separateth chief friends." Friends are lost, too, in the sharp competitions of business, in the keen rivalries of ambition; for love of money or of fame **or of** power or of social distinction many **throw** away holy friendships.

Friends are lost, too, by **death.** Often this process begins early; a child is bereft of father or of mother, or of both. All through life the sad **story** of bereavement goes on. As the leaves are **torn** from **the trees** by the rude storm, so are friendships plucked from our lives by Death's remorseless **hand.** There is something inexpressibly sad in the **loneliness** of old people who have survived the loss **of** nearly all their friends, **and who** stand almost entirely alone amid the gathering shadows of their life's eventide. Once they were rich in human affection. Children sat about their table and grew up **in their happy home;** many other true hearts **were** drawn **to** them along the years. **But one by** one their children are gathered home into God's bosom, until all are gone. Other friends—some in one way, and some in another—are also removed. **At** last husband or wife is called away, and one only survives of the once happy pair, lonely and desolate amid the ruin of all earthly gladness and the tender memories of lost joys.

Were it not for the Christian's hope, these losses of friends along the years would be infinitely sad, without alleviation. But the wonderful grace of God comes not only with its revelation of after-life, but with its present healing. God binds up his people's hearts in their sorrow and comforts them in their loneliness. The children and the friends who are gone are not lost; hand will clasp hand again and heart will clasp heart in inseparable reunion. The grave is only winter, and after winter comes spring with its wonderful resurrections, in which everything beautiful that seemed lost comes again.

> "God does not give us new flowers every year:
> When the spring winds blow o'er the pleasant places,
> The same dear things lift up the same fair faces:
>   The violet is here!
>
> "It all comes back, the odor, grace and hue—
> Each sweet relation of its life—repeated;
> No blank is left, no longing-for is cheated:
>   It is the thing we knew.
>
> "So, after the death-winter, must it be—
> God will not set strange signs in heavenly places;
> The old love will look out from the old faces—
>   My own, I shall have thee."

We come to the end, also, of many of our life's visions and hopes as the years go on. Flowers are not the only things that fade; morning clouds are not the only things that pass away; sunset splendors are not the only gorgeous pictures that vanish. What comes of all childhood's fancies, of youth's day-dreams and of manhood's and womanhood's vision-fabrics? How many of them are ever realized? Life is full of illusions. Many of our ships that we send out to imagined lands of wealth to bring back to us rich cargoes never return at all, or, if they do, only creep back empty with torn sails and battered hulks. Disappointments come to all of us along life's course. Many of our ventures on life's sea are wrecked and never come back to port; many of our ardent hopes prove only brilliant bubbles that burst as we grasp them.

Yet if we are living for the higher things—the things that are unseen and eternal—the shattering of our life's dreams and the failures of our earthly hopes are only apparent losses. The things we can see are but the shadows of things we cannot see. We chase the shadow, supposing it to be a reality; it eludes us and we do not grasp it, but instead we clasp in our hand that invisible thing of which the visible was only the shadow. A young man has his visions of possible achievement and attainment; one by one, with toil and pain, yet with quenchless ardor, he follows them. All along his life to its close bright hopes shine before him, and he continues to press after them with unwearying quest. Perhaps he does not realize one of them, and he comes to old age with empty hands—an unsuccessful man, the world says—yet all the while his faith in God has not faltered, and he has been gathering into his soul the treasures of spiritual conquest; in his inner life he has been growing richer every day. The struggle after earthly possession may have yielded nothing tangible, but the struggle has developed strength, courage, faith and other noble qualities in the man himself. The bright visions faded as he grasped them, leaving nothing but disappointment; yet if his quest was worthy, he is richer in spirit.

Thus, God gives us friends, and our heart's tendrils twine about them; they stay with us for a time, and then leave us. Our loss is very sore, and we go out bereft and lonely along life's paths. Even love seems to have been in vain, yielding nothing in the end but sorrow. It seems to us that we are poorer than if we had never loved at all; we have nothing left of all that was so precious to us. But we have not lost all. Loving our friends drew out to ripeness the possibilities of love in our own hearts; then the friends were taken away, but the ripened love remains. Our hearts are empty, but our lives are larger. So it is with **all our** experiences of disappointment **and** loss if our hearts are fixed on Christ and if we are living for the invisible things; we miss the **shadow only** to clasp **in** heart-possession the imperishable **reality.** The illusions of faith and hope and love **are but** the falling away of the rude scaffolding used in erecting the building, that the beautiful temple it**self** may stand out in enduring splendor.

We come also to the end of trials and sorrows. Every night has a morning, and, however dark it may be, we have only to wait a little while **for the sun** to rise, when light will chase away the gloom. **Every** black cloud that gathers in the sky and blots out the blue or hides the stars passes away ere long; and when it is gone there is no stain left on the blue **and not** a star's beam is quenched or even dimmed. The longest winter that destroys all life and beauty in field, forest and garden is sure to come to an end, giving place to the glad springtime which reclothes the earth in verdure as beautiful **as** that which perished. So it is with life's pains and troubles. **Sick**ness gives place to health. Grief, however bitter, is comforted by the tender comfort of divine love.

Sorrow, even the sorest, passes away and joy comes again, not one glad note hushed, its music even enriched by its experience of sadness.

> "No note of sorrow but shall melt
> In sweetest chord unguessed;
> No labor, all too pressing felt,
> But ends in quiet rest."

Thus in a Christian life no shadow lingers long. Then it will be but a little time till all shadows shall flee away before heaven's glorious light, when for ever life will go on without a pain or a sorrow.

There is another ending: we shall come to the end of life itself. We shall come to the close of our last day; we shall do our last piece of work, and take our last walk, and write our last letter, and sing our last song, and speak our last "Good-night;" then to-morrow we shall be gone, and the places that have known us shall know us no more. Whatever other experiences we may have or may miss, we shall not miss dying. Every human path, through whatever scenes it may wander, must bend at last into the Valley of Shadows.

Yet we ought not to think of death as calamity or disaster; if we are Christians, it will be the brightest day of our whole life when we are called to go away from earth to heaven. Work will then be finished, conflict will be over, sorrow will be past, death itself will be left behind, and life in its full, true, rich meaning will only really begin.

The criticalness of life should lead us to be always ready for death. Though we are plainly taught by our Lord not to be anxious about anything that the future may have in store for us, we are as plainly taught to live so as to be prepared for any event which may occur. Indeed, the only way to eliminate care from our present is to be ready for any possible future. Death is not merely a possible, but is an inevitable, event in every one's future; we can live untroubled by dread of it only by being ever ready for it. Preparation for death is made by living a true Christian life. If we are in Christ by faith, and then follow Christ, doing his will day by day, we are prepared for death, and it can never surprise us unready.

> "It matters little what hour o' the day
> The righteous falls asleep: death cannot come
> To him untimely who is fit to die.
> The less of the cold earth, the more of heaven;
> The briefer life, the longer immortality."

True preparation for death is made when we close each day as if it were the last. We are never sure of to-morrow; we should leave nothing incomplete any night. Each single separate little day should be a miniature life complete in itself, with nothing of duty left over. God gives us life by days, and with each day he gives its own allotment of duty— a portion of his plan to be wrought out, a fragment of his purpose to be accomplished by us. Says F. W. Faber, "Every hour comes with some little fagot of God's will fastened upon its back." Our mission is to find that bit of divine will and do it. Well-lived days make completed years, and the years well lived as they come make a life beautiful and full. In such a life no special preparation of any kind is needed; he who lives thus is always ready. Each day prepares for the next, and the last day prepares for glory. Susan Coolidge writes:

"If I were told that I must die to-morrow—
  That the next sun
Which sinks should bear me past all fear and sorrow
  For any one,
All the fight fought, all the short journey through—
  What should I do?

"I do not think that I should shrink or falter,
  But just go on,
Doing my work, nor change nor seek to alter
  Aught that is gone,
But rise and move and love and smile and pray
  For one more day;

> "And, lying down at night for a last sleeping,
>   Say in that ear
> Which hearkens ever, 'Lord, within thy keeping
>   How should I fear?
> And when to-morrow brings thee nearer still,
>   Do thou thy will.'"

If we thus live, coming to the end of life need have no terror for us. Dying does not interrupt life for a moment. Death is not a wall cutting off the path, but a gate through which passing out of this world of shadows and unrealities we shall find ourselves in the immediate presence of the Lord and in the midst of the glories of the eternal home.

We need have only one care—that we live well our one short life as we go on, that we love God and our neighbor, that we believe on Christ and obey his commandments, that we do each duty as it comes to our hand, and do it well. Then no sudden coming of the end will ever surprise us unprepared. Then, while glad to live as long as it may be God's will to leave us here, we shall welcome the gentle angel who comes with the golden joy to lead us to rest and home.

THE END.

www.ingramcontent.com/pod-product-compliance
Lightning Source LLC
Chambersburg PA
CBHW030808230426
43667CB00008B/1118